Plants, Stars, and the Origins of Religion

Plants, Stars, *and the* Origins of Religion

with a decipherment of the Phaistos Disk

Mary Kilbourne Matossian

Mill City Press
Minneapolis, MN

Mill City Press, Inc.
322 First Avenue N, 5th floor
Minneapolis, MN 55401
612.455.2293
www.millcitypublishing.com

ISBN-13: 978-1-62652-934-2
LCCN: 2014911174

Cover Design and Typeset by Sophie Chi

Printed in the United States of America

Contents

Figures

For the use of these images, the author gratefully acknowledges the following sources:

Fig. 1: Wikimedia Commons, public domain. Original source: Stephen Laymon, Department of Land Management, US Department of the Interior. **Figs. 2–4:** Alexander A. Marshack (1972), *The Roots of Civilization: The Cognitive Beginning of Man's First Art, Symbol and Notation* (New York: McGraw-Hill), 198, 223, 238. Permission granted by Peabody Library, Harvard University. **Figs. 5–6, 9–10, 19:** James Mellaart (1967), *Çatal Hüyük: A Neolithic Town in Anatolia* (New York: McGraw-Hill), 107, 123, 184; Pls. 13, 18. Permission granted by Çatalhöyük Research Project. **Figs. 7–8, 13, 16, 18:** International Astronomical Union and *Sky & Telescope* magazine (Roger Sinnott & Rick Fienberg), Creative Commons Attribution 3.0 Unported license. The author also acknowledges the kind assistance of Richard Dibon-Smith, *The Constellations,* dibonsmith.com. **Fig. 11:** Wikimedia Commons, public domain. Original image: J. H. Kirkbride, Jr., C. R. Gunn, and M. J. Dallwitz (2006) *USDA Family Guide for Fruits and Seeds,* version 1.0. **Fig. 12:** Mary Kilbourne Matossian (1980), "Symbols of Seasons and the Passage of Time," *Griffith Observer* 44 (11), 12–13, after a copy by Mrs. G. Huxtable, first published 1963 in *Anatolian Studies* 14, 65. Permission granted by British Institute at Ankara. **Fig. 15:** Y. Enzel et al., "Late Holocene Climates of the Near East deduced from Dead Sea level variations and modern regional winter rainfall," *Quaternary Research* 60:3 (2003), 263–73. **Fig. 20:** Photo by Kurt Stüber. Wikimedia Commons. Permission granted to use under GFDL by Kurt Stueber Source: [http://www.biolib.de www.biolib.de] {{GFDL}}.

The author wishes to thank her daughters, editor Lou Ann Matossian and artist Michele Matossian, for their assistance in the preparation of this book.

Introduction

Plants, Stars, and the Origins of Religion

Religion is a source of joy and relief from pain. The evidence so far suggests that it began to flourish around 35,000 B.C.E. in the caves of western Europe. A hallucinogenic drug may have been in use: wild plants and fungi helped to supply rapture to religion. People could drink their way to glory.

In Eurasia up to the time of Jesus and after there were scores of wild plants that yielded mind-bending (psychoactive) drugs. At least four, in simple form, had an important role in religion:

Claviceps paspali (ergot)
Vitis vitifera (wine)
Peganum harmala (wild rue) and
Papaver somniferum (opium)

Both archaeology and evolutionary psychology offer promising scientific approaches to the origins of religion. Psychologists study the human brain, seeking the fundamental nature of religion, which is a cultural universal. They ask, why do so many people believe in the supernatural?

A religion begins in a particular place at a particular time. For each religion these circumstances are different. Archaeologists try to determine the datable events that mark innovation and change in religions.

For over a century Western archaeologists have been studying the development of Upper Paleolithic art in Europe, 35,000–14,000 years ago. At the beginning of that period, people created the paintings on the walls of the Chauvet Cave in southern France, near the mouth of the Rhone River. This prehistoric art apparently marked the beginnings of the shared social beliefs and practices we call religion.

The cave paintings expressed awe with regard to certain wild animals (Whitley 2009, 196–7, 206–7). For this reason, the earliest stage of religious development has been called "zoomorphic."

Recently archaeologists have interpreted this Paleolithic art in relation to the religious beliefs and practices of archaic people surviving in modern times. These people are foragers, that is, hunters and gatherers, as were the Paleolithic artists. Contemporary foragers also revere animals.

The approach of this book is like that of the archaeologists. But I continue the story after the invention of writing in Mesopotamia in the fourth millennium B.C.E. (before the common era) until the Roman Empire of the first century C.E. (the common era), including the appearance of Jesus.

There is a widespread misunderstanding today that religion is all about morality. Religious leaders use religious beliefs to justify moral rules. But moral rules are probably older than religion. All social mammals have social rules; otherwise they could not bond and live together to their mutual benefit.

The basis of morality, a sense of fairness and the ability to feel compassion, probably goes back to the first hominids and social mammals. These creatures lived millions of years before the emergence of modern humans and their various religions.

Religion appeared in western Eurasia c. 35,000 B.C.E., only after the human brain reached a sufficient level of cognitive development. By that time, humans were able to integrate enough information to conceive of the world as an organization, or cosmos. They could also conceive of the human body as a whole.

Religion as a Natural Phenomenon

Psychoactive plants and fungi enabled people to have mystic, or ecstatic, experience. The availability of such plants and fungi varied from one environment to another, and in accordance with seasonal and climatic changes.

Because the supply is unreliable, psychoactive plants and fungi in the wild are only potentially addictive. Only when people settled down and cultivated these substances was there a continuous supply, sufficient to addict a significant number of people.

Ingesting a psychoactive substance was not the only way to bring on a trance or ecstatic experience. Other paths to ecstasy included sensory deprivation in dark caves and repetitive singing and dancing. But certain plants and fungi, when and where available, tend to provide ecstasy more reliably and quickly. In various parts of the world today, notably in Latin America, archaic people have continued to drink their way to glory. Their practices have helped us to imagine how prehistoric people around the world could have done the same.

On account of the work of the archaeologist David Lewis-Williams and others, there is considerable evidence that the European cave artists were hallucinating at least part of the time as they worked on their murals.

The Humanization Period, c. 3500 B.C.E. to c. 1000 B.C.E. (Chapters Four through Seven), is exemplified by ancient Mesopotamian, Egyptian, Minoan, and Greek religions. Human figures personified the various gods and goddesses, who represented the varieties of power in the world. These human-like beings were mostly amoral. The senior male was dominant, but his power was often limited by that of other deities. These deities usually had astral and animal associates.

In this period beer, wine, and opium were in widespread use. The mysterious drink *kykeon,* of the cult of Demeter, was apparently a hallucinogen. It may have been similar to *hamra*, the red drink of the Mandaeans of Iraq, or the *haoma* of the ancient Iranians (see Chapter Eight).

The Moralization Period, c. 1000 to the first century C.E. (Chapters Eight and Nine). The chief god in western Eurasia was seen as both all-powerful and purely good. His jurisdiction was universal. He lived in the sky, and all other gods were his servants. The goddesses faded or were redefined as angels and female saints.

In order to explain the existence of evil in the world, people imagined an evil deity (Satan, Shaitan, Eblis, Belial, etc.), who lived in the underworld. Hence, the term "monotheistic," often used to characterize such religions, is not entirely appropriate. At the time of moralization, a religious narrative predicted that all evil would end on a certain day, when the world ended and the good, living and dead, went to Heaven. But that lay in the future.

References

Atran, Scott. 2002. *In Gods We Trust: The Evolutionary Landscapes of Religion.* Oxford: Oxford University Press.

Barber, Elizabeth W., and Paul T. Barber. 2004. *When They Severed the Earth from the Sky: How the Human Mind Shapes Myths.* Princeton, N.J.: Princeton University Press.

Boyer, Pascal. 2001. *Religion Explained: The Evolutionary Origins of Religious Thought.* New York: Basic Books.

D'Aquili, Eugene G., and Andrew Newberg. 1999. *The Mystical Mind: Probing the Biology of Religious Experience.* Minneapolis: Fortress Press.

Dennett, Daniel. 2006. *Breaking the Spell: Religion as a Natural Phenomenon.* New York: Viking.

De Waal, Franz. 2006. *Primates and Philosophers: How Morality Evolved.* Princeton, N.J.: Princeton University Press.

Dornan, Jennifer. 2004. "Beyond belief: religious experience, ritual, and cultural neuro-phenomenology on the interpretation of past religious systems," *Cambridge Archaeological Journal* 4:25–36.

Gilligan, Ian. 2007. "Neanderthal extinction and modern human behavior; the role of climate change and clothing," *World Archaeology,* 39 (4):499–514.

Hauser, Marc D. 2006. *Moral Minds: How Nature Designed Our Sense of Right and Wrong.* New York: Harper.

Hayden, Brian. 2003. *Shamans, Sorcerers, and Saints.* Washington, D.C.: Smithsonian.

Hillman, D. C. A. 2008. *The Chemical Muse: Drug Use and Roots of Western Civilization.* New York: St. Martin's Press.

Lewis-Williams, David. 2009. "Of People and Pictures: The Nexus of Upper Paleolithic Religion, Social Discrimination, and Art." In *Becoming Human: Innovation in Prehistoric Natural and Spiritual Culture,* edited by Colin Renfrew. 135–58. Cambridge: Cambridge University Press.

———. 2010. *Concerning God: The Cognitive Origin and Evolution of Religion.* London: Thames and Hudson. 144.

Lieberman, Philip. 2007. "The Evolution of Human Speech: Its Anatomical and Neural Basis." *Current Anthropology* 48 (1):39–53.

Mithen, Steven. 1996. *The Prehistory of the Mind.* New York: Thames and Hudson.

Newberg, Andrew B. 2005. "Neuroscience and Religion." *Encyclopedia of Religion,* 2nd ed., vol. 10. 6485–95.

Whitehouse, Harvey. 2004. *Modes of Religiosity; A Cognitive Study of Religious Transmission.* Walnut Creek, Calif.: Altamira Press.

Whitley, David S. 2009. *Cave Paintings and the Human Spirit: The Origin of Creativity and Belief.* Amherst, N.Y.: Prometheus.

Chapter One

Hallucinations and Paleolithic Religion

Cave Art and Shamanism

The beginning of religion in western Eurasia may be found in the art that appeared in Chauvet Cave, near Lyon, France, possibly as early as 35,000 years ago or as late as 26,000 years ago. Discovered at the end of 1994, this may be the oldest cave art known today, with highly skilled renderings of mostly large animals such as reindeer, red deer, bison, horses, ibex, and aurochs (wild cattle).

Were these portrayals a form of hunting magic? The bones found in the cave indicated that the people's diet consisted mainly of small animals. This evidence suggests that the large animals in cave art were symbols, not a menu.

A prominent school of archaeologists, led by David Lewis-Williams and David S. Whitley, believes that these pictures are religious in nature. They may have been drawn by hallucinating artists under the influence of psychoactive drugs, trance dancing, or prolonged confinement in the darkness of the cave.

Along with the animals, the cave art includes part-human, part-animal figures. These can be understood in the light of shamanistic traditions still practiced today. The man is the healer of a foraging band or clan. The animal is his supernatural alter ego, or spirit helper. When the shaman in his trance hallucinates, he may see the form of his spirit helper and imagine that he has been transformed, that he has become one with that helper. The hybrid man-animal image on the cave wall is that of the shaman transforming himself (Whitley 2009, 38 and 43).

From this evidence we can infer that shamanistic practices surviving in modern times may have originated in religious beliefs and practices of the High Paleolithic Period (36,000–14,000 years ago) in western Eurasia. The cave art of the period shows that the shamans had organized their religious beliefs. Apparently, the human brain had by that time achieved the cognitive basis for such organization.

The beginning and end of High Paleolithic cave art in western Eurasia coincided with the appearance and disappearance of certain climatic conditions. Cave art appeared in a cool period: the glaciers had advanced. The average temperature ranged from –2° C (28° F) in winter to 12° C (53.6° F) in summer. Although there were as yet no deep forests, the abundant rain allowed grasses and other low-growing steppe and tundra vegetation to flourish, supporting large herds of wild animals. The humans too increased and multiplied. They created religious shrines in caves, which were lavishly decorated by masterful artists (Mellars 2009, 212–231).

Cave art featuring wild animals contains no spatial framework: no grass, no trees, and no horizon. The images appear suspended in air. The prehistoric artists may have envisioned the animals as living in a spirit world that was (in fact) a product of the imagination alone. Or perhaps, like some hunter-gatherers today, they considered the spirit world to be in the sky.

Paleolithic people probably imagined that some groups of stars represented animals. This is suggested by ancient, widespread traditions of bear worship on the northern edge of Northern Hemisphere continents. In this circumpolar region, the Great Bear and Little Bear constellations are at the center of the sky overhead and visible year-round.

Bears	Ursa Major and Ursa Minor
Horse	Pegasus
Bull	Taurus
Lion	Leo
Man	Orion

Table 1. Possible Astral Sources of Cave Art. The human and animal imagery of European cave painting and artifacts may have been inspired by bright constellations, or conversely, early peoples may have seen in the constellations human and animal images on earth (Condos 1997).

Zodiac, a word of Greek origin, signifies '(the circle) containing living creatures'. Of the twelve constellations in the sun's ecliptic, seven are animals: the ram, bull, crab, lion, scorpion, goat, and fish. Indeed, most of the major constellations, especially in the Northern Hemisphere, are animals, such as bees (the Pleiades), eagle, bear, horse, dog, swan, lynx, and snake.

The brightest constellation is Orion, the hunter. During the Paleolithic era, hunting was the main occupation of most men. It would have been natural for them to see in the celestial hunter a permanent illuminated reflection of themselves.

The brilliance of the sun, moon, stars, and planets must have deeply impressed early human beings. Unlike most earthly objects, celestial bodies constantly radiated light. People came to imagine the sky as the abode of gods and a part of the "spirit world." The sun, moon, and stars were also helpful to prehistoric people, serving as clock, calendar, and compass, especially in hot weather when it was necessary to travel by night (Krupp 1991, 3).

Shamans sought to attain an ecstatic state, believing that this consciousness gave them the power to heal and make predictions (Eliade et al. 2005, 8269–8293). Such individuals were found worldwide and used similar behavioral and biochemical techniques. The former included chanting, drumming and dancing, meditation, fasting, and other austerities. The biochemical technique was to ingest extracts of psychoactive plants and fungi. During his training the shaman often imagined that he had died, was dismembered, reconstituted, and reborn.

Through these techniques the shaman tried to take a "magic flight" to the "spirit world." Hallucinogens sometimes gave him the sensation of weightlessness and movement. He sought to recover lost souls of the living that had been seized and possessed by evil spirits. In small communities the shaman and his pupils were often the only ones who sought rapture, but elsewhere the whole community might join in the chanting and dancing.

Psychoactive Plants and Fungi

The skill of identifying natural hallucinogens, typically part of shamanistic lore, is as ancient as the human race. In a review of the ethnopharmacological literature, Kyoto University primatologists Don Cousins and Michael Huffman (2002) note that gorillas and chimpanzees in the wilds of West Africa ingest psychoactive plants. Gorillas eat the shrub *Tabernanthe iboga* (Apocynaceae), "an essential component in African religious cults and rites, particularly in Bwiti." Both gorillas and chimpanzees also enjoy *Alchornea floribunda* and *A. cordifolia* (Euphorbiaceae), which contain the alkaloids alchornine and alchornidine. The *Alchornea* drug, known as *alan* (pl. *malan*), was also used in the Bwiti rituals of a number of tribes, notably the Fang, in Gabon and the Congo (Samorini 2002, viii).

Apes ingest psychoactive plants that may have been available for millennia. Hominids in Africa evolved from an ancestral primate or primates who likely enjoyed the same substances. "Our earliest hominid ancestors can be predicted to have exhibited some similarities in plant selection criteria with both extant apes and modern humans," Cousins and Huffman conclude. What's good for one primate is often good for another.

"Plant hallucinogens in one form or another have been part of the human experience from the beginning," writes anthropologist Marlene Dobkin de Rios. Psychoactive drugs have been used in "all forms of society up to and including complex agricultural societies with formal government and monotheistic religion" (Dobkin de Rios 1984, 217; 2005, 7468).

Walter Burkert, an authority on Greek religion, said:

> Since the sacred, the divine, always appears as out of the ordinary, and wholly other, the overwhelming experiences of a changed and extended consciousness are, if not the sole origin, at least one of the most essential supports of religion. The experience may rest on natural disposition, acquired technique, or the influence of drugs… (Burkert 1995, 109).

Mark D. Merlin has noted the "ubiquity" of mind-altering agents in archaic societies, which associated those agents with ritual and/or religious activities (Merlin 2003, 295).

After years of studying Paleolithic art and the beliefs and practices of South African hunter-gatherers, David Lewis-Williams concluded that the creators of this art sometimes worked in an altered state of consciousness. Without specifying *which* psychoactive plants might have been involved, he said that religion is the result of brain functioning "in both natural and induced (man-made) conditions" (Lewis-Williams 2005, 26).

Lewis-Williams studied geometric patterns which appeared normally and cross-culturally in the early stages of a hallucinatory experience. Such patterns were called "entoptic phenomena." Common types were a grid or lattice, sets of parallel lines, bright dots, zig-zag lines (angular or undulating), nested chain-like curves, filigrees, and spirals. He matched these patterns with those found in Paleolithic art. Previously some art historians had dismissed them as mere doodles; now they seemed more significant.

Lewis-Williams said that the content of consciousness was mainly culturally mediated. However, the fact of common cross-cultural content in Paleolithic art indicated that the human brain was hard-wired in certain respects (Lewis-Williams 2005, 26, 43, 48, 51–55, 68, 122).

In his cross-cultural study, *Shamanism: Archaic Techniques of Ecstasy,* Mircea Eliade found that many shamans of North Asia and Siberia ingested the hallucinogenic mushroom *Amanita muscaria,* (fly agaric) in their rituals. Other shamans, in Iran, Scythia, and Thrace, used hemp (*Cannabis sativa*) to alter their state of consciousness (Eliade 1964, 103–104, 228, 390–39).

No one as yet knows what psychoactive substance, if any, the Paleolithic cave artists consumed. However, the mobile art of the Magdalenian Period (18,000 to 10,000 years ago) at the end of the High Paleolithic Age, contains some drawings that suggest this possibility. In examining them, it may be useful to remember that the Upper Paleolithic artists had the skills to render natural objects in a very realistic manner. Magdalenian workers produced points (microliths) which made it possible to draw fine-lined designs on bones and antlers.

Before the invention of writing, they probably tried to express their ideas by making pictures and diagrams as people still do today. One can therefore interpret their drawings on the basis of what is known about Paleolithic life as shown by research.

The work of Lewis-Williams et al. suggests that Paleolithic artists may have been familiar with hallucinogens, either by personal use or by observing others. If so, then it is likely that these artists wanted to record how, when, and where to find the substance that caused dramatic experiences of transformation and rebirth.

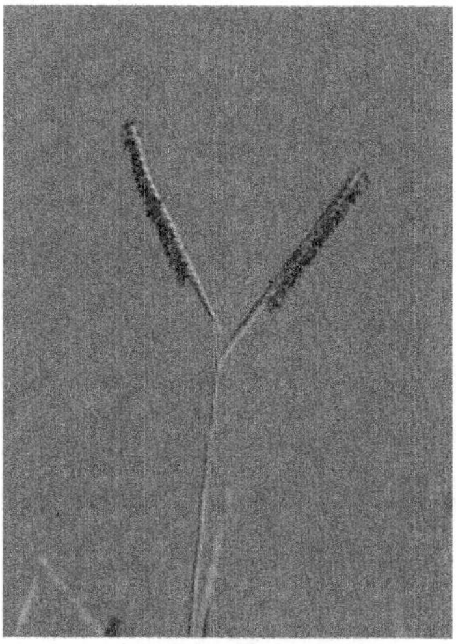

Figure 1. Knotgrass (*Paspalum distichum*).

Since the Paleolithic artists lived in or near grassy plains, and the glacial climate of the time provided abundant rain in spring, let us suppose that the hallucinogen of interest came from *Claviceps paspali,* an ergot fungus that colonizes wild grasses in wet spring weather. In spring the infected grass is easily distinguished by its bright yellow color against a bright green background of uninfected grass. Approaching the bright yellow grass, the artist would see at close range numerous small bulges (sclerotia) attached to the bright yellow stems, but not to the green blades.

"Claviceps" ("key-headed") refers to the shape of the sclerotia on a grass stem: protuberances projecting from the stem at an angle, like the business end of a key. In the case of *Claviceps paspali,* the protuberance is globular.

"Claviform" ("key-shaped") is the technical name given to the shapes in Figure 2 by archaeologists specializing in Paleolithic art.

The claviform (key-like) sign common in High Paleolithic art may represent the yellow sclerotia, packed with ergot alkaloids, attached to a grass stem. So far the similarity between claviform signs in cave art and the form of the genus *Claviceps* in nature has escaped attention.

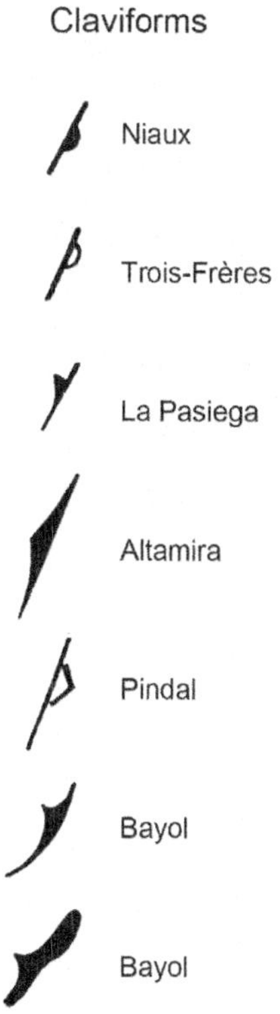

Figure 2. Paleolithic claviform symbols.

Now let us look at two diagrams carved on bony material of the Middle or Late period of Magdalenian culture in southern France.

Figure 3. Snake with two lines of globules, Upper Paleolithic mobile art. Alexander A. Marshack (1972), The Roots of Civilization: The Cognitive Beginning of Man's First Art, Symbol and Notation (New York: McGraw-Hill), 223.

Figure 3 shows a piece of antler engraved with a snake. Grass symbols have been placed over its neck. Above and below the snake are two rows of encased globular figures. To the right of some globes is an opening through which the figure may emerge from its case.

Interpretation: The snake, which periodically sheds its skin, can symbolize transformation and rebirth, the experiences sought by shamans when they took a hallucinogenic drug. Snakes hibernate in cold climates, and their reappearance is a sign of spring. Likewise, the sclerotia of *Claviceps paspali* emerge from their casing and fall to the ground. Spring is the time to harvest them.

In Figure 4 a bear's head is followed by lines that might represent cut grass, followed by two globular units.

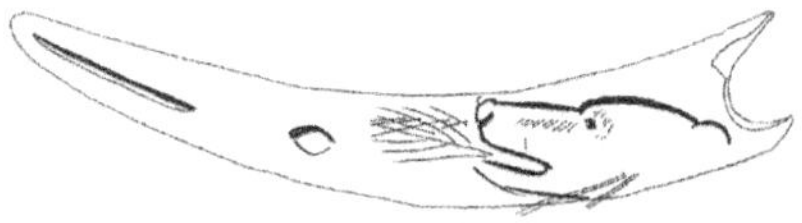

Figure 4. Bear with grass, globule and stem, Upper Paleolithic mobile art.

Interpretation: The bear has awakened (has been "reborn") and it is spring, time to gather the yellow grass. Look for the stems colonized by *Claviceps paspali.*

Were Paleolithic people intelligent enough to identify such an "ordinary" globular shape by sight and to link its ingestion with hallucinations? "It seems reasonable to assume that early hominids would have displayed at least the range of extant ape self-medicative behaviors," especially after the advent of language to communicate experiences about plant properties (Cousins and Huffman 2002, 74).

As shown in myths, humans inspired by the Milky Way thought that these beings were rotating in a great churn full of milk. Some imagined a whirlpool in the starry "ocean." Plato imagined a "Spindle of Necessity" around which the stars moved by threads.

String, Ropes, and Religion

Paleolithic women were never depicted as part animal. Their power evidently came from other sources, such as the ability to bear and nurture a child, find useful plants, and to convert vegetable fibers into rope, nets, and fabric (Hardy 2008, 271–280).

As anthropologists have recently confirmed, High Paleolithic people, probably female, understood that vegetable fibers became stronger when twisted (twined) into thread, string, and cords. Twisting is part of an operation called spinning. The word "string" is derived from Latin *stringere,* to bind tight; the word "strong" probably comes from the same root.

Two kinds of twist were used: the S-twist, from right to left; and the Z-twist, from left to right. Our ancestors made rope by twisting strings together with the S-twist to make cords, then twisting several cords with Z-twist to prevent them from unwinding. In 1953 the 15,000-year-old imprint of a fossilized rope of this kind was found in Lascaux Cave in France.

By 2001 anthropologists had discovered that as early as 26,000 years ago, sophisticated and diverse textile and cordage technologies had developed on the European plain from France to Russia. The evidence consisted of impressions of fabrics and cords on hardened substances, of charred remains, and of lines incised on carved female figures to indicate clothing (Soffer et al. 2000, 812–821; and 2001, 233–245). Where there is cloth, there must be weaving; where there is weaving there may be thread or yarn; and where there is thread or yarn there must be spinning.

As yet anthropologists have not determined the nature of the vegetable fiber used in the Paleolithic period. All vegetable fibers are perishable. However, educated guesses about their identity may be made.

Perhaps the best source of natural vegetable fiber for cords and rope is hemp. Its fibers may reach twelve feet long, compared with four feet for flax, a few inches for wool, and even less for cotton. The longer the fiber, the easier it is to twist and the stronger the cord that is likely to result. The remains of hemp have been found in Taiwan in a site dated 8,000 years ago, at the end of the Paleolithic period there (Merlin 2003, 307–308).

When people started using hemp they must surely have encountered the psychoactive contents of the hemp plant, *Cannabis sativa.* When harvesting seeds from the female plant they would get sticky resin on their fingers. If they licked their fingers they were likely to feel peculiar sensations. A brew from the harvested parts of the plant would produce stronger sensations. The product, as millions now know, was hashish. In this way, perhaps, humans discovered that hemp has another kind of power beside its tensile strength.

In myths one finds the idea that the binding and loosening of ropes held together the cosmic order. Ropes bound the heavens to the underworld. Ropes bound the celestial bodies to the central axis of the cosmos and influenced their courses. By means of a rope, the gods descended to earth and shamans ascended to heaven.

The Sumerians believed the earth and sky were bound together by a rope that served as a means of communication between heaven and earth. The god who held the cosmic rope controlled the universe as surely as a man might control an animal on a lead rope or a boat moored to a dock (Snell 2005, 322).

The Sumerians revered the bright planet Inana (Venus), which, hanging close to the horizon at dawn or at sunset for most of the year, was "moored." The earliest symbol of Inana was a hitching post with a ring near the top. By comparison with other stars and planets, this one rarely moved. The presence of a rope was implied (Black and Green 1992, 53 and 74).

In the Bible, God says to Job, "Do you bind the ties of the Pleiades or do you loosen the ties of Orion?" (Job 38:31). Jesus tells Peter, "What you shall bind on earth shall be bound in Heaven" (Matt. 16:19). Ropes, symbolically, were a means to establish and maintain the spiritual and moral order. The act of binding transformed chaos into cosmos (Rappengluck 2003, 89–92).

This may serve to explain why a shaman relied on a sacred rope as a symbol of the axis connecting earth and the "spirit world" above. Many believed that once upon a time, the earth and sky were linked by a rope which was later cut. A Bushman shaman dreamed of a "rope of light"—the Milky Way—as a passage to where he could see the gods and talk to them. In Tibet, it was believed that after death the king ascended a rope up into the sky.

The mythical "Indian rope trick" begins with the illusion that a rope is rising high into the sky. A disciple climbs up the rope until he disappears from view. Then the master throws his knife in the air and the disciple's "limbs" fall to the ground one after another. Later the disciple reappears, alive and whole.

> Similar stories can be found in the folklore of several countries and in the mythology of several cultures. Part of the appeal of the story of the rope trick may lie in its incorporation of two classic mythical themes—the astral cord connecting heaven and earth, and death and resurrection—which are so common among different cultures that they could be seen to represent fundamental themes in the human imagination (Lamont and Wiseman 2001, 188; see also Lamont 2004; Eliade1964, 428–430).

Orthodox Hindu males at the time of their initiation received a "sacrificial string (thread)." For a youth of the Brahmin caste it had to be made of three cords of cotton spun by a Brahmin girl, and twisted into a rope by a Brahmin adult male. It had to be as long as the breadth of a man's four fingers, times ninety-six. For a member of the warrior class, the cord was made of hemp; for a member of the merchant class it was made of wool. The initiation ceremony was called the *upanayana*. During the ceremony the boy's guru draped the "sacred thread" (i.e. cord) over his left shoulder and wrapped around his waist and tied it to a girdle of triple cord (Walker 1968, 498–501). Similar practices have been noted among the Zoroastrian Parsees of India, the animist Veddas of Sri Lanka, and the Christian Armenians (Arpee 1946, Villa and Matossian 1982).

The prehistoric notion of sacred binding may serve as a clue to understanding the word "religion," from the Latin verb *religere*, to bind again. Perhaps the practice of religion was originally understood as the way to maintain the spiritual and moral order.

References

Arpee, Leon. 1946. *A History of Armenian Christianity from the Beginning to Our Own Time*. New York: Armenian Missionary Association of America.

Barber, Elizabeth Wayland, and Paul T Barber. 2004. *When They Severed Earth from Sky: How the Human Mind Shapes Myth*. Princeton: Princeton University Press.

Burkert, Walter. 1985. *Greek Religion*. Cambridge. Mass.: Harvard University Press.

Charbrand, Leon. 2005. "Bears." In *Encyclopedia of Religion*, edited by Lindsay Jones, Mircea Eliade, and Charles J. Adams. 2nd ed., vol. 2, 806–810. Detroit: Macmillan Reference USA.

Clarke, Robert C. 1998. *Hashish!* Los Angeles: Red Eye Press.

Condos, Theony. 1997. *Star Myths of the Greeks and Romans: A Sourcebook.* Grand Rapids, Mich.: Phanes Press.

Cousins, Don, and Michael A. Huffman. 2002. "Medicinal Properties in the Diet of Gorillas: An Ethno-pharmacological Evaluation." *African Study Monographs* 23 (2): 65–89.

De Santillana, Giorgio, and Hertha von Dechend. 1977. *Hamlet's Mill.* Boston: Godine Press.

Dobkin de Rios, Marlene. 1984. *Hallucinogens: Cross-Cultural Perspectives.* Albuquerque, N.M.: University of New Mexico Press.

———. 2005. "Psychedelic Drugs." *Encyclopedia of Religion*, vol. 11, 7462–7473.

Eliade, Mircea. 1964. *Shamanism: Archaic Techniques of Ecstasy.* Princeton: Princeton University Press.

Eliade, Mircea, Michael Winkelman, and Anna-Leena Shkala. 2005. "Shamanism." *Encyclopedia of Religion*, vol. 12, 8269–8287.

Hardy, Karen. 2008. "Prehistoric String Theory: How Twisted Fibers Helped to Shape the World," *Antiquity* 82 (316): 271–280.

Harner, Michael J., ed. 1973. *Hallucinogens and Shamanism.* Oxford: Oxford University Press.

Hayden, Brian. 2003. *Shamans, Sorcerers, and Saints: A Prehistory of Religion.* Washington, D.C.: Smithsonian Books.

Johnston, Sarah I. 2005. "Hekate." *Encyclopedia of Religion*, vol. 6, 3899–3900.

Krupp, E. C. 1991. *Beyond the Blue Horizon: Myths and Legends of the Sun, Moon, Stars and Planets.* New York: HarperCollins.

Lamont, Peter, and Richard Wiseman. 2001. "The Rise and Fall of the Indian Rope Trick." *Journal of the Society for Psychical Research*, 65: 175–191.

Lamont, Peter. 2004. *The Rise of the Indian Rope Trick: How a Spectacular Hoax Became History.* New York: Thunder's Mouth Press.

Lewis-Williams, David. 2002. *The Mind in the Cave: Consciousness and the Origins of Art.* London: Thames and Hudson.

———. *Inside the Neolithic Mind: Consciousness, Cosmos, and the Realm of the Gods.* 2005. London, Thames and Hudson.

Marshack, Alexander. 1972. *The Roots of Civilization.* New York: McGraw-Hill.

Mellars, Paul. 2009. "Cognition and Climate." 212–231. In *Becoming Human.* Edited by Colin Renfrew and Iain Morley. Cambridge; New York: Cambridge University Press.

Merlin, M. D. 2003. "Archaeological Evidence for the Tradition of Psychoactive Plant Use in the Old World." *Economic Botany* 57 (2): 295–323.

Narr, Karl J. 2005. "Paleolithic Religion." *Encyclopedia of Religion*, vol. 10, 6948–6955.

Rappengluck, Barbara. 2003. "The Power of Binding and Loosening: Ropes Establish the Cosmic Order." 89–92. In *Calendars, Symbols, and Orientations: Legacies of Astronomy in Culture*, ed. Mary Blomberg, Peter E. Blomberg and Göran Henriksson. Uppsala, Sweden: Uppsala Astronomical Observatory.

Raynal, G. 1996. "Presence in France of *Claviceps paspali* Stev. et Hall on *Paspalum distichum* L. and of the Corresponding Ergotism in Cattle." *Cryptogamie, Mycologie* 17: 21–31.

Rudgley, Richard. 1998. *The Encyclopedia of Psychedelic Substances.* New York: St. Martin's Press.

Samorini, Giorgio. 2002. *Animals and Psychedelics.* Rochester, Vt.: Park Street Press.

Soffer, Olga, et al. 2000. "Paleolithic Perishables Made Permanent." *Antiquity* 74, 812–821.

———. 2001. "Perishable Technologies and Invisible People." 233–245. In *Enduring Records*, edited by B. Purdy. Oxford: Oxbow Books.

———. 2004. "Recovering Perishable Technologies Through Use Wear on Tools: Preliminary Evidence for Upper Paleolithic Weaving and Net Making." *Current Anthropology* 45: 407–413.

Villa, Susie Hoogasian, and Mary Kilbourne Matossian. 1982. *Armenian Village Life Before 1914.* Detroit: Wayne State University Press.

Wagner, Ron. 2005. "Totemism." *Encyclopedia of Religion*, vol. 5, 9250–9253.

Walker, Benjamin. 1968. *The Hindu World.* vol. 2, 498–501. New York: Praeger.

Chapter Two

Wine, Opium, and Neolithic Religion

The Neolithic period is defined as a time when people began to settle permanently and live by growing food crops. In the Fertile Crescent of the Middle East, village farming began around 9500 years ago. It continued around 3500 B.C.E., when towns and civilization began. In southeastern Europe people began to farm c. 7000 B.C.E.

The new lifestyle helped people to survive seasons of food scarcity. They did more and better spinning and weaving. They produced ceramic vessels for preparing, storing, and serving food and drinks. Some villages also grew psychoactive plants, notably wine grapes and opium.

Indeed the production of psychoactive drugs from plants and fungi may have been a more important motive for some agriculturalists than the production of food. There were many alternative wild foods that could sustain human life, but few if any plants in a given area could produce ecstasy. In the wild, food of some kind was usually available year round. But specific psychoactive plants fungi were available for only a limited period and in a limited amount.

Many people in different places had the opportunity to cultivate psychoactive plants. In some cases people could store the precious harvest and have a continuous supply all year. In that case the cultivators had to settle down to watch over their crops and storehouses.

Religion and the Agricultural Revolution

In 1994 the French archaeologist Jacques Cauvin published *Naissance des divinités, naissance de l'agriculture* (*The Birth of the Gods and the Origins of Agriculture,* 2000), in which he argued that a change in religious symbols occurred *before* the adoption of permanent settlements in the Middle East. He believed that this cultural change *encouraged* permanent settlement. Just why, he does not explain.

At that time, when domestic cattle played little or no role in the economy, The *wild bull* and a *goddess* figure appeared together as important symbols in the Levant and soon after, in Anatolia. Cauvin believed that this was a "restoration" of virility symbols (wild bulls) as opposed to female symbols in the religion of agricultural settlements (Cauvin 2000, 66 and 128). His work has been welcomed by Ian Hodder, chief excavator at the important Neolithic site of Çatal Höyük in Turkey, and other archaeologists who are critical of the work of the feminist archaeologist Marija Gimbutas.

Professor Gimbutas identified a religion of "the Goddess" among peoples of Eastern Europe and Southern Russia during the Neolithic period. She concluded the theme of their religion was eternal transformation: the reconstruction of life, rebirth, and renewed growth. A tripartite female deity, Hekate or the Three Fates, symbolized this idea in Greek times (Gimbutas 1989, 316–321).

Astral Influence on Neolithic Iconography: Çatal Höyük

The most famous Neolithic settlement in the Middle East is Çatal Höyük near Konya, Turkey. The site was inhabited from c. 7400 to 6200 B.C.E. Cessford 2001, 721). Çatal Höyük has an excellent location for observing the night sky. It is located on a plain 84 miles to the east of the twin-coned volcano: Hasan Dagh (3,235 meters,) and Kara Dagh (2271 meters). The slot between the twin peaks is a possible reference point for the rising and setting of celestial bodies.

In the art of Çatal Höyük there was a goddess and a wild bull, the bull predominating. The goddess was not paired with a god in human form, as in ancient Mesopotamia. The bull was not paired with a cow as in ancient Egypt. Why was a female human associated with a male animal at Çatal Höyük?

By inspecting the images so far unearthed at Çatal Höyük one may find a number of indications of astral influences. This can be done by virtual reconstruction of the sky over Çatal Höyük at the time when it was inhabited. The dates chosen for virtual observation were 7065 B.C.E., near the beginning of settlement and 6345 B.C.E., near the end. All observations were made with the use of the computer program Starry Night Pro, which was corrected by backdating two months (May 22 = March 21).

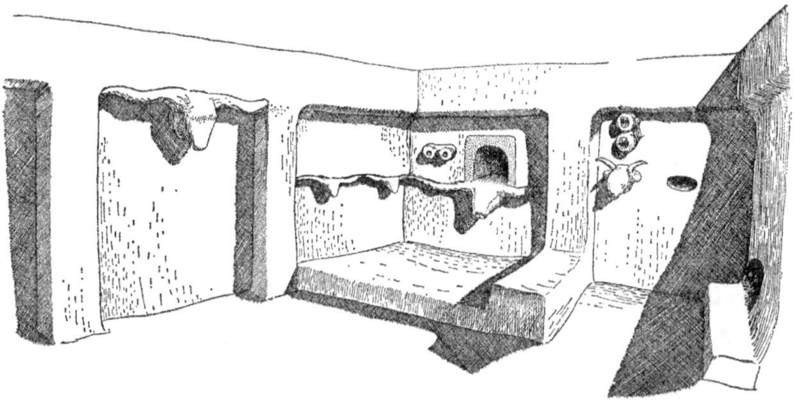

Figure 5. Bulls' heads, ram's head and woman's breasts, Çatal Höyük.

The *bull's head* was ubiquitous at Çatal Höyük. Some bull muzzles were decorated with designs.

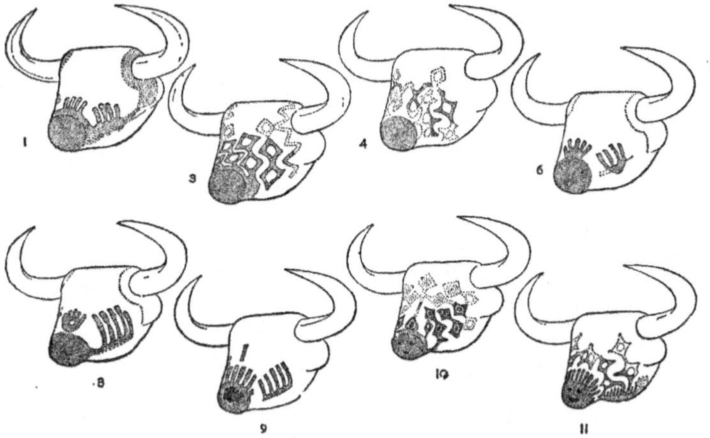

Figure 6. Bulls' heads with decorated muzzles, Çatal Höyük.

Overhead Taurus, the zodiac constellation, is in a region of the sky full of bright stars. The constellation is distinctive for its triangular head, the muzzle of which is studded with a cluster of bright stars known as the Hyades.

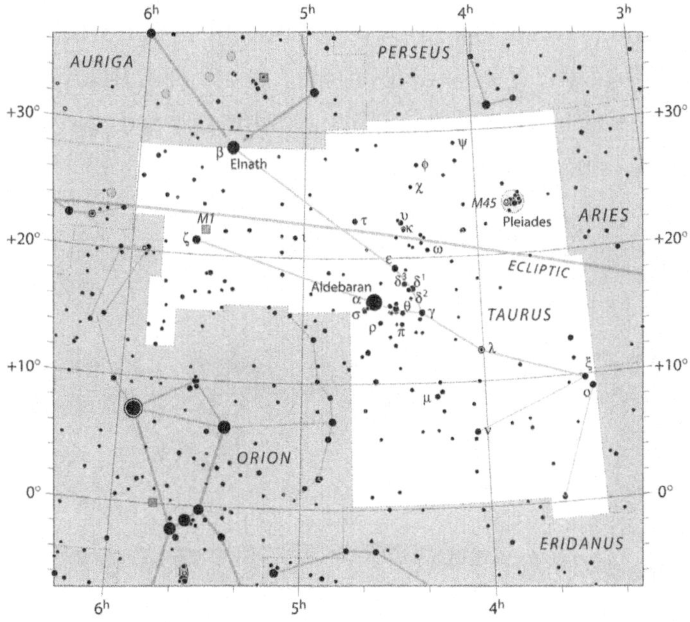

Figure 7. The constellation Taurus.

2. *The head of a smaller horned animal* was on display next to that of the bull. The horns of the animal point upward, forming a V.

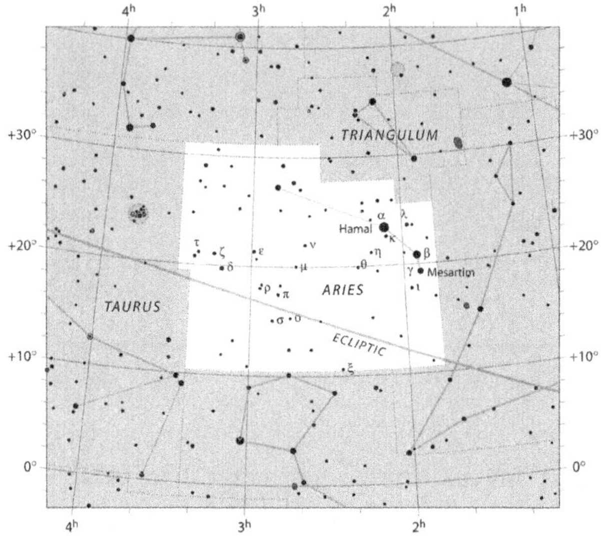

Figure 8. The constellation Aries.

In the sky next to Taurus was the zodiac constellation of Aries, currently interpreted as a ram's head. But the ram horns in nature curl backward. The V resembles more a goat head. In any case, the horns of the animal at Çatal Höyük point upward and outward, forming a V—like those of Aries.

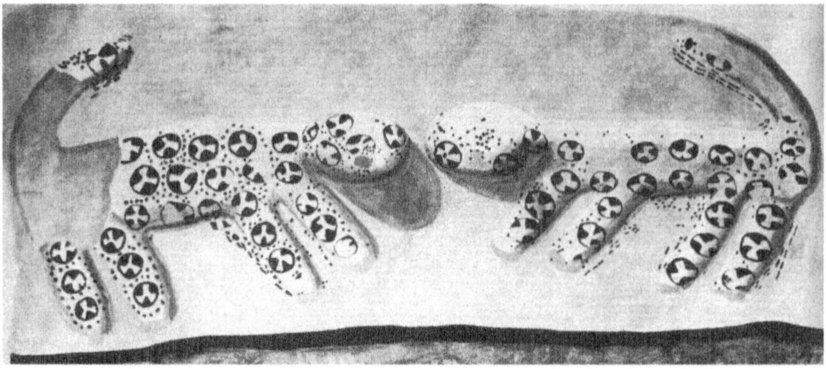

Figure 9. Leopards with trefoil figures, Çatal Höyük.

3. "*Leopards*" decorated with trefoil spots were found in pairs alone and in association with a pregnant goddess at Çatal Höyük. In several cases the spots were white on a black background. Leopard spots are black on a tawny background. Why place white figures inside them?

Stars are usually portrayed as white on a black background. Could this be a starry "leopard"?

Professor Ian Hodder has said that the spotted "leopard" might be a "symbolically decorated dog," among other possibilities. Knowing that leopards are intensely solitary animals, he suggested that the pair of identical leopards facing each other might not represent two animals, but both sides of one animal in mirror image. How did the people of Çatal Höyük imagine the opposite side of an animal? Hodder knew the existence of polished obsidian mirrors at Çatal Höyük that reflected images well (Hodder 2006, 229). The pair of leopards might have been in fact the ordinary image and the mirror image of a leopard.

Hodder was puzzled that in the portion of Çatal Höyük already excavated (5%), 65% of the paintings and 35% of the reliefs were of "leopards;" but none of the "faunal remains" (mostly bones) were those of leopards. Belatedly Hodder was elated by the discovery of one tiny bone from a leopard's claw (Hodder, 2006, 9, 11, 91). He did not suggest the possibility that the "leopard" portrayed repeatedly at Çatal Höyük was not a terrestrial but a celestial creature.

If some of the leopard's spots represented stars, which stars? Which constellation? One must look for one or two quadrupeds that contain bright stars.

A possible match for the "leopard" might be the constellation known as Canis Major. The "Great Dog" is studded with bright stars, notably Sirius, magnitude 1.5, the brightest star in the sky. Could this constellation have been interpreted as a leopard at Çatal Höyük?

Canis Major had a smaller partner, Canis Minor, which contains another very bright star, Procyon.

When Çatal Höyük was an occupied site, for most of the year Canis Major was invisible below the southern horizon. Its chief star, Sirius, appeared at dawn at the end of May, underneath the constellation Gemini. By July 22 Canis Major was completely visible at dawn, but it never rose very much above the horizon. It set at the end of September. This beast may have appeared, consequently, as being "under control." It may have inspired the statuette of a pregnant woman seated with her hands on the heads of a pair of felines on each side of her, as if controlling them.

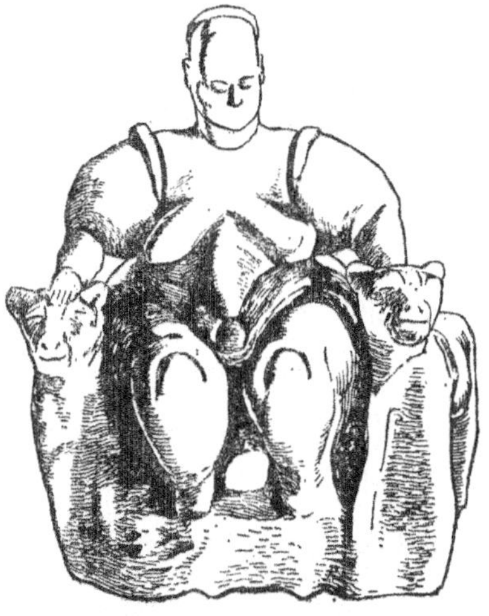

Figure 10. Goddess with two felines, Çatal Höyük

It may be the inspiration for the later Greek and Minoan "Mistress of Animals."

The Mistress of Animals is controlling a pair of animals, however. One is not a mirror image of the other. What constellation could the second animal be?

Why not Canis Minor, including the bright star Procyon (magnitude 0.34), the eighth-brightest star in the sky? That constellation, too, appears beneath Gemini and is not far from Canis Major. Two spotted dogs, two spotted leopards; they are under the control of a woman, in this interpretation. (In Hindu mythology, the Mother Goddess rides on a lion or a tiger.)

Why were many of the leopard's spots in the shape of a trefoil? This is not a common shape in nature. However, the seed pod of the plant *Peganum harmala* (wild rue) is trefoil in shape. Its seeds contain psychoactive alkaloids which can, in a tea, induce a state of calm elation. James Mellaart identified this plant, "ruin weed," growing on the site of Çatal Höyük (Mellaart 1967, 27). While the trefoil leopard spots may represent the trefoil-shaped fruit of *Peganum harmala*, the quadrifoil spots may represent the quadrifoil shape of the opium poppy.

4. *A female dancer* appeared in the company of a bull's head and sometimes the smaller horned animal's head as well. Both her arms and legs were stretched out to the sides. The legs can be called splayed. Mellaart said, "This goddess is shown with her head and body in profile, her long locks floating behind her" (Mellaart 1967, 116–117).

Figure 11. Trefoil-shaped seedpod of wild rue (*Peganum harmala*).

This female figure may represent a whirling dancer, her hair blowing in the wind. She recalls the origin myth of the Pelasgians, people who lived in Greece before the arrival of the Greeks. According to the Pelasgian creation myth a cosmic dancer once stood on the *axis mundi* and constantly rotated.

According to the Pelasgians, in the beginning, Eurynome, a cosmic dancer brought the whole universe into being. In India she was called Nataraja.

The Hindus also had an androgynous cosmic dancer called Shiva, a pre–Indo-European deity and an important Hindu deity today. As this deity whirls around and around, his/her hair blows outward into the sky. Shiva is both destroyer of evil and creator of good. Shiva is also associated with *two hallucinogens, hashish and datura*. A third cosmic dancer revered in India is Kali, thought of as dark and destructive, but also as bright.

Now, as the result of more advanced investigative technology, evidence of beer and wine production has appeared in residues in jars of the Neolithic period. The discipline of paleoethnobotany (the study of plants used by ancient peoples) has also assumed an important place in archaeology.

The most advanced study is that of ancient wine. Dr. Patrick McGovern of the University of Pennsylvania uses DNA analysis to determine the ancestry of grape cultivars. He uses liquid chromatography (HP-LC) the chemical compound in complex mixtures. He uses infrared spectrometry to identify particular molecules, especially those of tartaric acid found in residues at the bottom of Neolithic ceramic containers. Tartaric acid is a product of wine decomposition.

Much progress in wine research has been made in former Anatolia (now Turkey). Wild grape seeds dated 9000 B.C.E. have been found at Çayönü. Agriculture began there c. 8000 B.C.E. Pottery, necessary for the production, storage, and convenient consumption of psychoactive drinks, appeared in the Middle East in 7,000 B.C.E. Grape cultivation and winemaking began in the highland plateaus of Anatolia, Transcaucasia, and Northern Iran by 6000 B.C.E.

According to Genesis 8:4 and 9:2, Noah's Ark landed on the peaks of Mount Ararat (in Armenia). Once he had disembarked, Noah planted a vineyard. This tradition suggests that the cultivation of the grapevine began in Armenia. There are Neolithic sites there that still have not been excavated.

Moderate wine consumption may have contributed to human survival. The polyphenolic aromatic compounds in wine have antiseptic properties. There are antioxidants in wine that scavenge free radicals in the body, lower cholesterol, and protect against cancer. Moderate consumption of wine relieves stress by releasing natural pleasure compounds, endorphins and encephalines, in the brain.

One of the advantages of using grapes for fermentation is that the natural bloom on grapes is yeast, *Saccharomyces cerevisiae.* It is not necessary to add a yeast to grape juice (must): the grapes carry this natural fermentation agent as a bloom on their skins.

Beer (produced by slow fermentation) and ale (produced by rapid fermentation) required a grain supply. Barley was typically used since it was hardier than wheat and lacked the gluten needed to make bread. The processes include malting, which is the controlled germination of grain; mashing, which is the conversion of starches into malt sugar; and fermentation, which is the conversion of sugars into alcohol. Both beer and ale were produced in the Neolithic Near East (Dineley 2004, 19–26; Jacobsen 1976, 62).

Neolithic Opium

In the latter part of the nineteenth century C.E. archaeologists found abundant evidence of opium cultivation in Neolithic Europe. In the sixth millennium B.C.E. it was cultivated in abundance in the Swiss foreland. Subsequently other evidence was found in Neolithic Spain, Italy and Central Europe. It had been thought that knowledge of opium did not reach the Middle East until the late third millennium (Merlin 1984, 110–120, 168–174; Booth 1996). However, during his 1962 excavations at Çatal Höyük, James Mellaart uncovered a mural which he described as a honeycomb pattern (Mellaart 1963).

The 78-cell pattern looks like the growth cycle of a plant, starting from the planting of seeds on the left to the blooming of flowers on the right. There are also flowers mixed with insects on the right. This mural was located at Level VI. This is significant because the first ceramic pottery found in the site so far appeared at that level (Hodder 2006, 86). Opium could not have been boiled without ceramic containers.

Figure 12. Mural, Çatal Höyük.

An alternative explanation, that the mural represents the development of honeybees, is not tenable, because the hatching period for bees (16, 24, 27 days) depends on the function of the bee; and the life term of the bee varies both by the function of the bee and the season.

In column 21, cell 48 of the mural is a flower that resembles an opium poppy: it has four petals and a dark spot on each petal near the center.

In cell 29 is a six-unit design, suggesting the usual six septa in the crown of opium poppies grown in Turkey. An analysis of this mural suggests that the people of Çatal Höyük were growing these poppies in the late seventh millennium B.C.E.

Opium poppies grow from tiny seeds. The spring poppies in Turkey today are sown in late February or March and their growth cycle is forty to sixty days. In Turkey they usually flower at the end of April or early May, and have four petals. The flowers last four to five days, and then their petals fall. The seed capsules grow for ten more days and then they are ready to harvest.

The poppies exude a heavy perfume which makes the harvesters dizzy and sometimes gives them a headache. The collected capsules must be gently incised with a knife to allow the sap to come out. The sap has to be boiled, filtered, and simmered to attain full potency.

It has been suggested that prehistoric peoples grew poppies just for their seeds, which were abundant and nutritious. However, it would impossible to extract the seeds from the opium poppy seed capsules without getting sticky sap on one's fingers. If the harvesters licked their fingers, they would likely feel dizzy and perhaps inebriated. It is unlikely that anyone harvesting opium poppy capsules would be unaware of their psychoactive potential.

The alkaloids present in opium include morphine and codeine. Both are very addictive, especially morphine. They depress the central nervous system directly, relieving pain and coughing. They also relieve anxiety and fear, producing euphoria. After an opium-induced sleep, there is no hangover: the user feels subdued and calm. Opium is both pleasant and very addictive. That is why it is so dangerous.

The crown of the poppy seed capsule may have four to eighteen septa, depending on the altitude at which it is grown. Poppies grown at low altitudes, such as Mesopotamia, have a larger number of septa (eight) than those grown at higher altitudes in Turkey (six). The number of poppy petals is four or eight (United Nations Technical Section, 1950). The original poppy color is believed to be white with a purple spot deep inside each petal (Merlin 1984, 17). The honey bee is very sensitive to shades of blue and purple (Ellis 2004, 22–23).

Bees play a dual role in connection with the opium poppy. The bees pollinate the poppies. They also produce honey, which can serve as a solvent and sweetener for opium. Pure opium is very bitter to taste and if ingested alone can cause severe nausea and vomiting. But it is palatable if mixed with a sweetener, and the main sweetener available in prehistoric and ancient times was honey. Opium also can be ingested comfortably when mixed with wine or mead (fermented honey).

The life of honeybees also follows a cycle. The bees hibernate in the late fall and winter. They wake up in the spring close to the spring equinox, March 21. At the latitude of Çatal Höyük *the period from March 21 to the swarming of bees was forty-eight days.* The swarming of bees would be about May 9, 11, or 13, alternate dates for the Roman Day of the Dead (Columella 1954, 481–483). In ancient times honey was poured as a libation to the dead on such holidays (Ransome 1937, 120).

Decipherment of the Honeycomb Mural

Returning to the Çatal Höyük mural, the writer decided to "read" it left to right, as suggested by James Mellaart, because this reading followed the pattern of plant growth. She decided to read the columns from up to down, since that is how objects move in response to gravity.

Across the top of the mural is a sequence of pairs of hands inside almond-shaped mandorlas, the fingers pointing at each other. There are fifteen hands of four fingers each: total = 60. The hands stop at Cell 47, the day before the usual swarming date of bees. The top level hands start on the left side of the mural *before* Cell 1, suggesting that they pertain to the bee life cycle instead of the poppy cycle.

On the bottom of the mural are other hands, alternately turned upward and sideways. The hands get larger and more prominent on the bottom right side of the mural, suggesting more manual labor is involved (in harvesting) than on the left side. There are ten groups of five fingers each (10 x 5 = 50) and 7 groups of four fingers each (7 x 4 = 28). Total = 78. This may represent the work time needed from preparing the ground, the planting of the poppy seeds, their flowering, and their ripening ten days later, the time for collecting the capsules. Counting the cells between the dark and bright crescents:

Group of Cells	**Total Cells in Group**
1–7	7
8–21	14
22–29	8
30–37	8
38–52	15
Cells of two concentric circles	8
Total	**60**

This table supports the view that the maker of the mural was counting in accordance with the lunar cycle of twenty-nine and a half days. The reason may have been that she believed that the growing moon promoted plant fertility: that the seeds grew better after the new moon when the moon was waxing. This is a widespread folk belief even today, a form of sympathetic magic (Frazer 1914, 132–150).

The mural may be a set of directions for the production of opium, coordinated with the actions of honeybees.

So, far archaeologists have found no botanical remains of the opium poppy at Çatal Höyük. But they have not reported any examination of the residues in jars. Moreover, at time of writing they have only excavated 5% of the ruins at the site.

References

Allen, Richard Hinckley. 1899. *Star-names and Their Meanings.* New York: Stechert.

Allouche, Adel. 2005. "Arabian Religion." In *Encyclopedia of Religion*, edited by Lindsay Jones, Mircea Eliade, and Charles J. Adams. 2nd ed., vol. 1, 442–446. Detroit: Macmillan Reference USA.

Baalbaki, Rohi. 2003. *Al-Mawrid: A Modern Arabic-English Dictionary.* 17th edition. Beirut: Dar el-Ilm Lil Malayin.

Bagley, Clinton. 1974. "Bedouin star lore in Sinai and Negev." *Bulletin of the School of Oriental and African Studies* 37: 580–596.

Bailey, Douglass W. 2005. *Prehistoric Figurines: Representation and Corporeality in the Neolithic.* New York: Routledge.

Barber, Elizabeth W. 1994. *Women's Work: The First 20,000 Years. Women, Cloth, and Society in Early Times.* New York: Norton.

Booth, Martin. 1996. *Opium, a History.* New York: St. Martin's Press.

Cauvin, Jacques. 2000. *The Birth of the Gods and the Origins of Agriculture.* Cambridge: Cambridge University Press. Originally published as *Naissance des divinités, naissance de l'agriculture: La révolution des symboles au Néolithique.* Paris: CNRS, 1994.

Cessford, Craig. 2001. "A New Dating Sequence for Çatal Höyük," *Antiquity* 75: 717–725.

Columella (Lucius Junius Moderatus). *On Agriculture (De Re Rustica).* 3 vols., 1941, 1954–1955. Translated by Harrison Boyd Ash, E. S. Forster, and Edward H. Heffner. Loeb Classical Library 361, 407–408. Cambridge, Mass., Harvard University Press.

Dineley, Merryn. 2004. *Barley, Malt and Ale in the Neolithic.* Oxford: Archaeopress.

Eliade, Mircea. 1958. *Patterns in Comparative Religion.* New York: Sheed and Ward.

Eliade, Mircea, and Laurence Sullivan. 2005. "Earth." *Encyclopedia of Religion*, vol. 4, 2554–2561.

Ellis, Hattie. 2004. *Sweetness and Light: The Mysterious History of the Honeybee.* New York: Harmony Books.

Fowler, W. Warde. 1899. *The Roman Festivals in the Period of the Republic: An Introduction to the Study of the Religion of the Romans.* London and New York: Macmillan.

Frazer, James George. 1962. *Adonis, Attis, Osiris.* 3rd edition. New Hyde Park, N.Y.: University Books. First edition 1906, London and New York: Macmillan.

Gimbutas, Marija. 1989. *The Language of the Goddess.* San Francisco: Harper & Row.

———. 1991. *The Civilization of the Goddess.* San Francisco: HarperSanFrancisco.

Graves, Robert. 1960. *The Greek Myths.* London: Penguin.

Haim, S. 1993. *Farsi (Persian)-English Dictionary.* New York: Hippocrene Books.

Herodotus. 1970. *The Histories.* Edited by Aubrey De Sélincourt and John Marincola. Translated by Aubrey De Sélincourt. Penguin Classics. London: Penguin Books.

Hodder, Ian. 2006. *The Leopard's Tale: Revealing the Mysteries of Çatalhöyük.* London: Thames & Hudson.

Jacobsen, Thorkild. 1976. *The Treasures of Darkness: A History of Mesopotamian Religion.* New Haven: Yale University Press.

Mallory, J. P., and Douglas Q. Adams. 2006. *The Oxford Introduction to Proto-Indo-European and the Proto-Indo-European World.* New York: Oxford University Press.

Matossian, Mary K. 1980. "Symbols of Seasons and the Passage of Time: Barley and Bees in the New Stone Age." *Griffith Observer* 44 (11), 9–17.

McGovern, Patrick. 2003. *Ancient Wine.* Princeton: Princeton University Press.

Mellaart, James. 1967. Çatal Hüyük: A Neolithic Town in Anatolia. New York: McGraw Hill.

———. 1963. "Excavations at Çatal Hüyük, 1962: Second Preliminary Report." *Anatolian Studies* 13: 43–103.

Merlin, Mark D. 1984. *On the Trail of the Ancient Opium Poppy.* Rutherford, N.J.: Farleigh Dickinson University Press.

Ransome, Hilda. 1937. *The Sacred Bee in Ancient Times and Folklore.* Boston and New York: Houghton Mifflin.

Russell, Nerissa, and Kevin J. McGowan. 2003. "Dance of the Cranes: Crane Symbolism at Catalhoyuk and Beyond." *Antiquity* 77: 445–455.

Schaefer, Bradley E. 2006. "The Origin of the Greek Constellations." *Scientific American* 295: 96–101.

Srejovic, Dragoslav. 2005. "Neolithic Religion." trans. Veselin Kostic. *Encyclopedia of Religion*, vol. 10, 352–360.

Steingass, F. 2006. *A Comprehensive Persian-English Dictionary.* New Delhi: Manohar Publishers.

Sweet, Louise E. 1960. *Tell Toqaan: A Syrian Village.* Anthropological Papers no. 14. Ann Arbor: University of Michigan Museum of Anthropology.

United Nations Technical Section. 1950. "The Cultivation of the Opium Poppy in Turkey." *United Nations Bulletin on Narcotics* 1: 13–25.

Varisco, Daniel M. 2000. "Islamic Folk Astronomy." In *Astronomy Across Cultures: The History of Non-Western Astronomy,* edited by Helaine Selin, 615–650. Dordrecht, Boston: Kluwer Academic Publishers.

Chapter Three

THE ANCIENT NEAR EAST, 3500–2200 B.C.E.

The Invention of Civilization: The Sumerians

The favorable warm climate of the Neolithic Period continued for another millennium.

During the second half of the fourth millennium B.C.E., the Sumerians invented civilization in Mesopotamia (Iraq). They created cities, writing, monumental architecture, complex irrigation systems, and city government. They invented the wheel and the first wheeled vehicles. They probably did so, in part, because they were under pressure.

Mesopotamia was chronically insecure. For protection it had the Syrian Desert to the west and the Arabian Desert to the south. But it was vulnerable to attacks from the mountains to the north (Tauros) and east (Zagros). The irrigation channels of Mesopotamia were often damaged by flooding.

The various city states of the Tigris-Euphrates Valley fought each other. Each had its favorite deities. But the population was growing dense enough, and transport was growing efficient enough, for strong men to recruit followers in a wider area and expand their holdings.

The Sumerians in southern Mesopotamia had a complex economy which involved much contact with their neighbors. They had to import most of their metal (copper, tin and then iron), building stone, and timber. The mountainous areas to the north (Anatolia and Armenia) and east (Iran) had necessary metal ores. Cyprus and Crete were rich in copper.

The fastest way to travel, especially to transport heavy goods, was by water. The Sumerians could not sail up the Tigris and Euphrates because the winds were not favorable. They had to tow ships upstream, which took four times as long as floating downstream with the current. Then the Sumerians invented the wheel and built wagons to haul materials—upstream or wherever else. They also sailed with the monsoon winds through the Persian Gulf to and from India (Boss 1995, 1421–1426).

In the mid-fourth millennium B.C.E., the growth of government made it necessary to keep records of taxes paid in kind to the temples of important city gods. The Sumerians invented writing in order to keep economic records. Then the scribes began to record myths and tales. For the first time we have detailed knowledge of ancient religions.

All these changes in transportation and communication technology made possible the standardization and elaboration of religious thinking. Rulers could make conscious use of religion for political purposes.

The political context of religion changed. Some men specialized in military skills to defend the ruler (almost always a male) and his domain. The hunters of animals became the hunters of men. Hunting evolved into militarism.

Governments had an unfortunate weakness: the hunters of men had special access to the sacred drink, usually wine. Drunkenness at royal banquets was notorious, hangovers on the day of battle, a dangerous weakness. The use of opium by troops or sailors could lead to catastrophe.

Kingdoms, Animals, and Stars

The peoples of the ancient Middle East imagined many constellations in the form of animals. An important animal in historic Mesopotamia, as in Çatal Höyük, was the bull.

In the year c. 4310 B.C.E., the constellation Taurus rose at dawn on March 21, starting the Age of the Bull. It lasted until 2150 B.C.E. Bull worship extended around the Fertile Crescent. In early Sumeria the supreme sky god, Enlil, was represented by the bull Gugalanna, whose bellowing was the thunder. Marduk, chief god of Babylon, was represented also by a bellowing bull. The cult spread to Assyria, Persia, the Levant, and Egypt. In Egypt the golden calf and sacred bull were symbols of the sun. Baal, the storm god of the Canaanites, and the Hittite storm god Haddad were also represented by a bull. During the second millennium, bull sacrifice was important in Minoan Crete.

There were two other royal beasts. Lions were known for their size, strength, valor, ferocity, and dignity. Many kings adopted the king of beasts as their symbol. Another favorite royal creature was the eagle or falcon. This bird of prey was fierce, had keen eyesight, and flew very high in the sky.

Rulers used the symbols of the bull, the lion, and the eagle to intimidate people. These animals appeared either alone or in hybrid form, such that a bull or lion might be depicted with wings or a human head.

The first kings clearly wanted to be feared more than to be loved. So they chose predators, not benevolent creatures, to represent them (Hutton 2005, v. 8, 5464–5465 and Waida 2005, v. 2, 947–949). In addition, they could point to the sky and see the bull, the lion, and the eagle as the immortal constellations of Taurus, Leo and Aquila.

The dove was a different kind of creature: a messenger who was believed to carry messages from earth to sky and vice versa. This bird represented the soul after death (Waida 2005, v. 2, 947–949).

Columba, the dove constellation of the southern sky, hovered over the horizon about three months of the year.

Other Mesopotamian divinities associated with constellations were Shala (Virgo), The Good Shepherd of Anu (Orion), Enlil (Boötes), and Pabilsag, son of Enlil (Sagittarius). After the time of Hammurabi (1726–1676 B.C.E.), all the major Assyrian and Babylonian deities were assigned places in the heavens. Shamash was the sun; Sin, the moon; Ishtar, Venus; Marduk, Jupiter; Nergal, Mars; Nabu, Mercury, and Ninurta, Saturn. The beneficent planets Jupiter and Venus contrasted with sinister Mars and Saturn, while Mercury was seen as ambiguous.

In 1000 B.C.E. the Babylonian zodiac contained eighteen constellations, but by 400 B.C.E., it had been pared down to twelve, with thirty days assigned to each (Black and Green 1992, 190).

Religion for most Mesopotamians was mainly a matter of performing a ritual and making a sacrifice. Sacrifices to the gods maintained the priests of the gods. There were no complex theological doctrines (Snell 2005, 344).

The drinking of beer and wine, begun in the Neolithic period, continued in ancient Mesopotamia. Alcohol probably served as a welcome relief to the hardworking farmers, enhancing their religious festivities. Since alcohol was not a hallucinogen, however, it could not produce ecstatic experiences, such as out-of-body travel in a fantastic environment.

Inana was the Sumerian goddess of love and the planet Venus (as both morning star and evening star), the third-brightest celestial object after the sun and moon. As late as Biblical Roman times, her worship continued in the Near East under such names as Ishtar, Astarte, 'Attar, Ashtoreth, Aphrodite, Venus.

In artifacts these deities were associated with the rosette (Black and Green 1992, 17, 51, 156). This shape probably represented the crown of the opium seed capsule.

The rosette first appeared in Mesopotamia on a dish from Arpachiyah, northern Mesopotamia, in the sixth millennium B.C.E. (Settegast 2005, 8). It had 16 septa, a doubling of the probable eight septa on the crown of the Mesopotamian opium capsules. The doubling of the septa was probably an artistic device to fill the space on the large dish. In Sumeria the rosette again appeared as an emblem of Inana, usually involving eight septa (Figs. 3 and 4).

The eight-septa rosette, like the eight-pointed star of Inana, was also related to the planet Venus in that it took eight solar years for Venus to return to the place in the sky where it began.

An excellent example of the rosette is an artifact from Babylonia c. 1800 B.C.E. showing a goddess surrounded by six eight-septa rosettes. She holds two bottles in her hands. What was in them? She wears a crenellated crown similar to the crown on the poppy seed capsule. Perhaps the bottles held wine or honey in which the bitter opium sap was dissolved.

Inana, one of the earliest deities of the Sumerians, was not a mother goddess: she was never described as a responsible parent and helpmate. She was seductive and irresponsible and she destroyed her lovers in the end. Likewise, one who ingests opium and becomes its "lover" is destroyed in the end. Millions of morphine and heroin addicts today are evidence of this sad truth. But those who can use morphine to escape a painful death have reason to be grateful to the unknown Neolithic discoverers of opium.

The Mesopotamians were concerned about ethics. An Akkadian text condemned lying, slander, perjury, oppression of weak women, estrangement between father and son, contempt for parents and elder sister, cruelty to captives, cheating in commerce, trespassing, shedding the blood of a neighbor, and approaching a neighbor's wife (Buccellati 1995, 1688–89).

Ethical concerns played some role in Babylonian religion. The gods were believed to be just, and often angered. People thought that they should confess their sins completely and seek to atone for them. They believed that humility before the gods was a virtue. These were signs of the incipient moralization of religion. But the main focus of religion was to obtain favors from powerful supernatural beings.

The Egyptians

Civilization in Egypt began around 3100 B.C.E., four centuries later than in Mesopotamia. Upper Egypt (in the south) and Lower Egypt (in the north) were united by Narmer around 2920 B.C.E. There were struggles for the control of the country but it tended to stay united and secure. Deserts to the east and west and the sea to the north kept enemies out and restive subjects in. The Pharaohs claimed to be gods, sons of the sun, and created a state religion to fortify their authority.

Egypt was blessed by the Nile. On account of the prevailing winds that blew southward, sailing south against the current was not difficult. The ancient Egyptians traveled along the coasts of the eastern Mediterranean and by moving counter-clockwise they reached the Levant. Then they sailed west to Cyprus and Crete. They also sailed in the Red Sea as far as Somalia (Punt).

The Egyptian gods were associated with animals such as the bee (Neith), the cow (Hathor), the baboon and ibis (Thoth, god of scribes), the jackal (Anubis, god of the underworld), the lioness (Sekhmet, the warrior), and the falcon (Horus, the sky-sun god).

Many of the provinces of Egypt were identified with animals: the cobra, viper, hare, oryx, jackal, falcon, and crocodile in Upper Egypt, and the bull, cow, ibis, fish, and falcon in Lower Egypt. Animals served as totems, which were like the mascots used today by sport teams.

A peculiarity of Egyptian religion was that it personified the sky as a female goddess: Neith, Nut, and Hathor, and Isis were alternative deities. All four were probably pre-dynastic in origin. Hathor and

Nut were associated with the Milky Way. Isis was associated with Sirius, the brightest star in the sky. The rise of Sirius in summer signaled the annual flooding of the Nile.

Hathor was mistress of alcohol-facilitated merrymaking. The Egyptians, like the people of Mesopotamia, enjoyed wine and beer. The grapevine and barley were the sources of their recreational drinks.

The four Egyptian goddesses were associated with the sky. On the ceiling of the tomb of Sethor I in Thebes (1306–1290) several constellations were depicted, each with a pattern of stars upon the body of the creature portrayed. Hathor, portrayed as a cow, had only *two stars* on her body: one on the neck and the other on the rump. As noted in the chapter on Neolithic religion, the two bright stars most similar in magnitude and close enough to each other to be conceived as pair were Casper and Pollux in Gemini. This supports the idea that "Gemini" was once conceived as a female (Wilkinson 2003, 90–91).

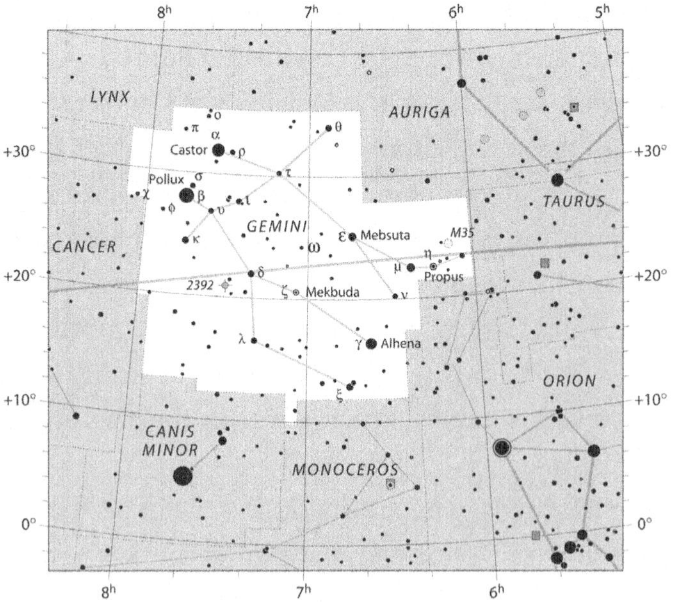

Figure 13. The constellation Gemini.

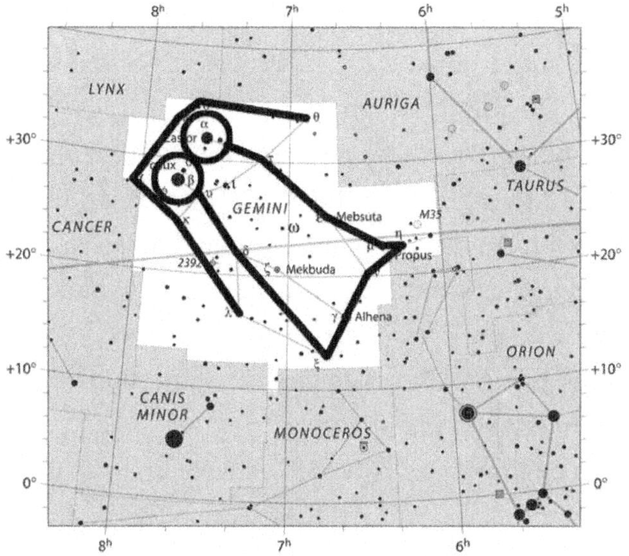

Figure 14. The constellation Gemini, redrawn by the author.

Nut was the personification of the whole vault of the night sky. The Egyptians believed that Nut's laughter was the thunder; her tears were the rain. They believed that Nut swallowed the stars at dawn and re-birthed them after sunset. The Minoans and Greeks apparently had a similar notion: when a star rose, they believed that the god it represented was "born" or "reborn." When it disappeared over the horizon it was seen as "swallowed" by some supernatural figure.

The Egyptians identified Venus with the morning star, and Saturn with the Bull of Heaven (Taurus). Mars and Jupiter were linked to Horus, the falcon. The Egyptians recognized the constellations Great Bear and Orion.

The unifying role of the Nile River and the protective deserts to the east and west of the Nile Valley served to support unified rule over the whole area. The Pharaohs were rulers of this area and extended their influence to the south and east from time to time, but they claimed no universal jurisdiction.

Some Egyptians spelled out moral precepts in writing. *The Book of Two Ways,* dated 2705–2706 B.C.E., called upon people to be honest. During the reign of Thutmose I, 1509–1497 B.C.E., in *The Book of the Dead (Going Forth by Day),* people were told to refrain from the following: theft, greed, murder, cheating, lies, trespassing, usury, gossip, adultery, defiling themselves (?), sex with a boy, quarreling, being abusive to the pharaoh, winking, wading in water, and raising the voice (Chapter one hundred twenty-five, the "negative confession"). But these moral injunctions were not well integrated into Egyptian religion.

Religions beginning in 3500 B.C.E. were primarily intended to bestow power, pleasure, and good luck upon their adherents. They served to unify communities and groups of communities. They provided occasions for drinking beer and wine. When people offered the gods sacrifices, the gods were expected to give favors in return.

We now turn to a Bronze Age Civilization on the island of Crete.

Minoan Civilization, 3000–1200 B.C.E.

Minoan Civilization was a Bronze Age civilization on the island of Crete. The Minoan form of writing, Linear A, has not been fully deciphered. The Minoans had a mercantile economy and with their large fleet they engaged in trade around the Mediterranean.

In Minoan art the number of women portrayed greatly exceeds that of men. Women are portrayed sitting on thrones and in commanding positions. They are saluted by people and animals. No woman is shown deferring to a man. The men are youthful, quite unlike the bearded warriors of Mesopotamia and Egypt.

Scholars agree that the central figure in Minoan religion was a powerful goddess of Nature. Her symbols were snakes and birds (like the Goddess in southeastern Europe) and poppies. In her association with opium she resembled the love goddesses of Mesopotamia and the Fertile Crescent.

The goddess was addressed only as *Potnia,* a term of respect like "Mistress" or "Madam." She had no male consort of equal or greater power. (For more on Minoan religion see Chapters Five and Six.)

Minoan civilization came to a dramatic end, variously dated 1500 and 1450 B.C.E. A tidal wave 46 meters high hit their coasts with a deafening roar. Other tidal waves followed. About four-fifths of the population lived in coastal cities, and almost all were drowned. Minoan civilization was nearly destroyed (Lilley 2007). In 1420 appeared the Mycenaean Greeks, who by 1200 occupied the whole island.

Judaism in the Iron Age

Israelis, eager to confirm the historicity of the Hebrew Bible, have conducted a great deal of archaeological work in Israel since the second half of the twentieth century. On the whole, though, they have been disappointed. They have found no confirmation for the existence of the patriarchs (Abraham, Isaac, and Jacob), of Joseph or Moses, or of their great kings, David and Solomon. It is not certain if their two small states, Israel and Judah were ever united.

After exploring the Sinai Israeli archaeologists have found no evidence of any Hebrew habitation there at the supposed time of the Exodus. What they have found is that the ancient Hebrew communities in the Land of Canaan were much like other Canaanite communities, both in material culture and religion. As a result many scholars have concluded that the Jews were never enslaved in Egypt, that there never was an exodus from Egypt. If the walls of Jericho fell, it was probably not the work of an army invading from the Sinai.

The new evidence suggests that the nucleus of the Jewish states came from the indigenous population of Late Bronze Age Canaanites. The true liberation of the Jews from the Egyptians came in 605 B.C.E. when the Egyptians, defeated in fighting the Babylonians, withdraw from Palestine.

Archaeological work, which began in 1929 at the site of ancient Ugarit at Ras Shamra on the coast of Syria, has provided a rich supply of information about the religion of the Canaanites. Their chief god was the sky patriarch El-Shaddai (Lord God), his wife was Asherah, and his son was Baal. El-Shaddai had a beard and sat on a throne.

The information from Ugarit has been used to interpret the passages which mention these deities in the Bible. From this material and other archaeological digs we find Venus, called Ashtoreth in Phoenicia and Attart in Ugarit. She was the goddess of both sexuality and war. She was associated with Friday, a sacred day for women in nineteenth-century Russia and eastern Europe.

According to the scholar Mark S. Smith, mention of the god Yahweh first appeared in western Asia at the beginning of the Iron Age, c. 1200 B.C.E. He was a warrior god of the southern Hebrew tribes. From 1200 to 1000 B.C.E. the chief Canaanite god El, his consort Asherah, and his son Baal were part of Israel's Canaanite heritage. In the ninth century B.C.E. the Jews began to reject the worship of Baal. In the eighth to sixth centuries they rejected Baal, Asherah, and sun worship. El and Yahweh were merged as a single god. For a time Asherah, as the consort of El, became the consort of Yahweh and together they looked after Israel.

The Ugarit materials reveal that Canaanite deities had an astral character, which cannot be found in the Hebrew Bible. They make references to "the assembly of the stars," and "the circle of those in heaven." The deities beside El, Asherah and Baal included the sun, the moon, dawn, dusk, and the planet Venus (morning and evening star).

The Canaanite gods, like those of Mesopotamia and Egypt, also had animal connections. The bull, cow, calf, and bird were benevolent. The snake was destructive. Astarte (Venus) was associated with the lion, horse, dove, and a star in a circle (the pentacle) (see references to wild rue) (Smith 2001, 32–33, 61, 141–142).

Mark S. Smith has argued that in the years of the Israelite kingdoms there were two groups: 1) those who worshiped and recognized Yahweh alone, and 2) those who worshipped only Yahweh but recognized that other gods existed as well (*monolatry*).

Monolatry was also found in Egypt and Mesopotamia. So was the idea of covenant between a god and his worshippers. The Jewish covenant with Yahweh was based on a formula in wide use in the second millennium B.C.E.

The Israelites were later convinced that only Yahweh existed and should be worshipped (monotheism). This development took place after 586 B.C.E., when the Babylonians, having defeated the Israelites in battle, destroyed their temple in Jerusalem, and took a large number of Israelites captive to Babylon. After the return from exile in 539 B.C.E., priests revised the Hebrew scriptures, so that they recognized only Yahweh as god (with a few exceptional passages). According to Dr. Smith,

> Monotheist claims made sense in a world where political boundaries or institutions no longer offered any middle ground. All nations around Judaea had a protective chief god. Egypt and Babylonia were larger and stronger states than Judaea. Monotheism was not a new stage of religion, but a new stage of rhetoric in a situation never known prior to the threat of exile (Snell 2005, 409–418; Smith 2005, 2995, 2033–2035; Smith 2001, 193; and "The Bible in History" in Wikipedia).

Most discussions of the origin of Judaism say nothing about the role of wine in its rituals. Judaism, like all the religions of the Middle East from Neolithic to Biblical times, was a "wet" religion. The Bible refers to wine 140 times. Every major event in Jewish life, including the beginning and end of the Sabbath, is marked by wine. One cup is allowed at a circumcision; two cups at a wedding, four cups at a

Passover *seder*, and ten cups at a funeral feast. Yahweh, like Dionysos, was a wine god (McGovern 2003, 236–237).

Thus, in the origins of Judaism we find a sacred plant (the grapevine), sacred animals, and gods associated with stars.

Religion and Politics in Ancient Kingdoms

From the above summaries of the religions of ancient Mesopotamia, Egypt, Minoan Crete, and Iron Age Judaea, we find some interesting traits in common.

First, the political context of all of them was a kingdom. These kingdoms expanded and contracted but did not achieve long-term imperial status. They lacked the population density, military technology, and transportation technology to rule such a large area. They also lacked a universal religion suitable for multi-ethnic consumption.

Second, the chief deity of these religions was powerful and sometimes just, but neither omnipotent nor merciful. Believers acknowledge the existence of other deities, just as they recognized the existence of other kingdoms. This involved recognition of the limited jurisdiction of secular authorities.

Third, the deities in these religions were more humanized that in the Neolithic, but less humanized than those among the Greeks and Romans to come. These religions and morality were only partially integrated.

Fourth, most deities had an astral and/or animal associate. The chief deity was often associated with the bull. There was a continuity from the Neolithic period to this period of kingdoms.

Fifth, wine was a sacramental drink, served at the festivals associated with these religions. Opium continued to be used by individuals. There was no indication of the use of hallucinogens at this time in the Fertile Crescent.

Sixth, all four religions served to unify the population of the kingdom and struggles with their neighbors. They did so by enhancing the power of the ruler. In Sumeria temples were used as warehouses for the king's taxes in kind.

In the next chapter we will consider influence of the Indo-Europeans on Middle Eastern religion. Like an invasive species, the Indo-Europeans changed the game both militarily and religiously.

References

"Astarte." Wikipedia.

"The Bible in History." Wikipedia.

Bass, George F. 1995. "Sea and River Craft in the Ancient Near East." In *Civilizations of the Ancient Near East,* edited by Jack M. Sasson, vol. 3, 1421–1431. New York: C. Scribner's, Simon & Schuster Macmillan.

Black, Jeremy, and Anthony Green. 1992. *Gods, Demons and Symbols of Ancient Mesopotamia.* Austin: University of Texas Press.

Brown, H. B. 1916. "Life History and Poisonous Properties of *Claviceps Paspali,*" *Journal of Agricultural Research* 7(9): 401–406.

Buccellati, Giorgio. 1995. "Ethics and Piety in the Ancient Near East." *Civilizations of the Ancient Near East,* vol. 3, 1685–1696.

Burroughs, William J. 2005. *Climate Change in Prehistory: The End of the Reign of Chaos.* Cambridge: Cambridge University Press.

Fagan, Brian. 2009. *The Great Warming: Climate Change and the Rise and Fall of Civilizations.* New York; Bloomsbury Publishing USA.

Gnoli, Gherardo. 2005. “Haoma.” In *Encyclopedia of Religion*, edited by Lindsay Jones, Mircea Eliade, and Charles J. Adams. 2nd ed., vol. 6, 3775–3776. Detroit: Macmillan Reference USA.

Hendel, Ronald S. 2005. “Israelite Religion,” *Encyclopedia of Religion*, vol. 7, 4742–4750.

Jacobsen, Thorkild, and Giovanni Pettinato. 2005. “Mesopotamian Religion.” *Encyclopedia of Religion*, vol. 9, 5946–5967.

Lesko, Leonard H. 2005. “Egyptian Religion.” *Encyclopedia of Religion*, vol. 9, 5946–5967.

Lilley, Harvey. 2007. “The Wave that Destroyed Atlantis.” BBCTimewatch, April 20.

Matthee, Rudi. 2005. *The Pursuit of Pleasure: Drugs and Stimulants in Iranian History, 1500–1900*. Princeton: Princeton University Press.

McGovern, Patrick E. 2003. *Ancient Wine: The Search for the Origins of Viniculture*. Princeton: Princeton University Press.

“Mesopotamian Religion.” Wikipedia.

“Minoan Civilization.” Wikipedia.

Pelon, Oliver, and Nanno Marinatos. 2005. “Aegean Religions.” *Encyclopedia of Religion*, vol. 1, 37–44.

Settegast, Mary. 2005. *When Zarathustra Spoke: The Reformation of Neolithic Culture and Religion*. Costa Mesa, Calif.: Mazda Publications.

Snell, Daniel C., ed. 2005. *A Companion to the Ancient Near East*. Oxford: Blackwell.

Smith, Mark S. 2001. *The Origins of Biblical Monotheism: Israel's Polytheistic Background and the Ugaritic Texts.* Oxford: Oxford University Press.

———. 1990. *The Early History of God: Yahweh and the Other Deities in Ancient Israel.* San Francisco: Harper & Row.

Westenholz, Joan G. 1998. "Goddesses of the Ancient Near East, 3000–1000 B.C." In *Ancient Goddesses: The Myths and the Evidence,* edited by Lucy Goodison and Christine Morris, 63–82. Madison: University of Wisconsin Press.

Wilkinson, Richard H. 2003. *The Complete Gods and Goddesses of Ancient Egypt.* New York: Thames & Hudson.

Waida, Manabu. 2005. "Birds." *Encyclopedia of Religion,* vol. 2, 947–949.

Chapter Four

A Time of Troubles, 2200–400 B.C.E.

Around the year 2200 B.C.E., the climate began to get dryer in the Middle East. This marked the beginning of a time of invasions, migrations, and an end to the relative security of the Age of the Bull.

The people who caused the most trouble were the Indo-Europeans, now believed to have spread out from a homeland in Anatolia. This conclusion is based on linguistic evidence, and is the work of a New Zealand team led by evolutionary biologist Quentin Atkinson. One branch of these people moved west and gave most Europeans their present language. Forks of this branch produced the Greek city-states and the Roman Empire. The east branch of Indo-Europeans moved south and eastward to Armenia, Persia, Afghanistan, and Northern India. That is why the languages of those "Asian" territories are akin to the languages of Europe. Both belong culturally in western Eurasia.

These successful invaders had military advantages: they had the use of domesticated horses and they possessed the chariot. They also may have had a secret chemical weapon: a hallucinogenic drink used in their religious rituals.

The Indo-Europeans

The social organization of the Indo-Europeans was patriarchal and patrilineal. At first they rode horses for managing their herds of cattle, horses and sheep, but did not ride in battle. Until 3200 B.C.E. they depended on lumbering carts with solid wheels.

In 2100 B.C.E. an unknown people in Central Asia acquired the chariot pulled by two to four horses. This chariot had spoked wheels, which were lighter than solid wheels, and which a horse could pull much faster. Chariots were introduced into the Middle East by way of Central Asia (Anthony 2007, 403–405).

The appearance of the chariot was a major military innovation. It gave a great advantage to men who could tame the horses to the point that they could be harnessed and controlled on the battlefield. At least two passengers were needed in the car of the chariot: one to drive the horses, and the other to shoot arrows and throw spears (Anthony 2007, 411). Later warriors rode horseback.

The invention of the chariot coincided with the end of the Age of the Bull and the beginning of the Age of Aries ("the Ram"), c. 2150 B.C.E. This was also the beginning of a time of drought, during which people left home and invaded neighboring countries.

The Indo-Europeans began to trouble the Middle East by 1800 B.C.E. Inhabitants of the two river valleys, the Nile and the Tigris-Euphrates, were relatively successful in limiting the incursions. This was because the river valley rulers promptly adopted the chariot technology of the invaders and used it to repel them. However, certain Indo-European tribes, notably the Greeks, Armenians, and Persians, came to stay and thrive in the ancient Middle East. Some of them learned to build large sailing ships.

The Indo-Europeans played a dramatic role in the history of religion. Their religion was more male-dominant and more aggressive than that of the earlier agricultural peoples of western Eurasia.

The original Indo-European myth of the origin of the cosmos, according to Bruce Lincoln, was that in the beginning there was a pair of male twins. Manu sacrificed his twin brother Yemo ("Twin"), the first king, along with the first ox, to the celestial father god. The whole world, both its material and social components, was made from the body of Yemo (see the "Song of Purusha" in the Rig Veda, dated c. 900 b.c.). The earlier mythologies did not feature a set of male twins. The constellation named Gemini (Twins) before the coming of the Indo-Europeans may have been known as The Central Woman (See Chapters Two, Five, and Six).

The Indo-Europeans were not the first to make religious use of a psychoactive substance: that practice, as has been shown, probably went back deep into prehistory, perhaps into the Upper Paleolithic. But the Indo-Europeans were the first people to create explicit records of this practice, first oral, then written.

The Indo-European drug, called *soma* by the Hindus, *haoma* by the Persians, was stimulating. Under its the influence, the Indo-Europeans had visions and experienced rapture. In contrast, the beer, wine, and opium of the Fertile Crescent farmers were tranquillizing.

The discovery of their hallucinogenic drink may have occurred while the Indo-Europeans were still confined to the Anatolia Plateau. Freezing temperatures prevailed for weeks in winter. During the rainy season, in spring and summer, grass grew in abundance. Herds of Indo-European cattle, horses, sheep and goats grazed on huge expanses of wild grass. All these animals produced milk. When the grasses were loaded with a globular fungus growing on their stems, so was the milk of the herds. In the spring there may have been plenty of the sacred drink to go around. There was no easy way to store this sacred milk for long, so addiction was unlikely.

The first written records mentioning the use of a hallucinogenic drug appeared in Iran and Northern India among the Indo-European conquerors of these areas. The Indo-European invaders of Greece who organized the cult of Demeter, c. 1500 B.C.E., may have served a hallucinogenic drink, *kykeon* (see Chapters Eight and Nine).

The Indo-Europeans of northwest India who composed the Rig Veda had to travel from the lowlands into the mountains to collect the essential component of their sacred drink. Only the alpine pastures could achieve the necessary low temperature for activating *Claviceps paspali* fungi.

Before the appearance of Zoroaster, the Persians worshipped an all-knowing ruler called Mithra, a "god of wide pastures." In a prayer to the god *Haoma*, the personification of the hallucinogen, the priest said "O Green One, I call down your intoxication, your strength, victory, health, healing, furtherance of increase, power for the whole body, ecstasy of all kinds." Apparently the word "green" referred to grass stems to which the hallucinogenic fungi attached themselves as rows of globules (Boyce 1984, 55 and 73–74). In India, a similar drink, *soma*, was described as yellow or yellowish. The sclerotia of *Claviceps paspali* (which contain the hallucinogen) are yellowish when picked, and when roughened they turn bright yellow (Brown 1916, 401).

The Indo-Europeans learned to pound the harvested material in a mortar, blending it with milk or curds. They added water and strained the mixture repeatedly through thick woolen cloth. Straining removed any solid pieces and toxic fatty elements, leaving the hallucinogenic ergot alkaloid in aqueous solution. The preparation process was known only to priests and was passed down by word of mouth.

The identity of the hallucinogenic ergot alkaloid occurring in nature is a matter of unresolved controversy. Mott T. Greene said (1992) that it was a lysergic acid amide of some kind. William Scott Shelley, in a personal communication (2008) suggested that it was lysergic acid hydroxylethylamide.

A relevant passage from the *Rig Veda* is: "We have drunk *soma* and become immortal; We have attained the light the Gods discovered. Now what may a foeman's malice do to harm us? What, O Immortal, mortal man's deception?"

The reference to light in this passage suggests that the drink caused the drinker's pupils to dilate. This condition, known as mydriasis, is induced by all hallucinogens, especially LSD, an ergot derivative (Lincoln 2005, Brereton 2005, Gnoli 2005, and Greene 1992, 106–137).

The ritual drink was for men only. This drug probably played an important role in the Indo-European conquests because the rituals served to bond warriors into groups large enough to overwhelm even well-organized agricultural peoples.

Another psychoactive plant of relevance here is one that grows in semi-arid places. Traces of *Peganum harmala* (wild rue) dating back earlier than the fifth millennium B.C.E. have been recovered in the Caucasus. This herb, which contains harmine and harmaline, became more common in the Middle East in the third millennium B.C.E. (Merlin, 2003, 301). In a relatively small dose, wild rue can produce a mood of calm elation, very useful for men going into battle. A near-toxic dose can produce hallucinations. Wild rue was probably taken in combination to intensify the effects of a true hallucinogen.

The chariot would not have made possible large-scale Indo-European invasions had the warriors lacked a means to bond with large numbers of other warriors. In the absence of a sacred drink and gods in common, the invention of the chariot might have only precipitated more costly tribal warfare and feudalism. Technological innovation was a necessary, but not sufficient, cause of large-scale Indo-European aggression.

Another factor predicting warfare is climate change. Historically, steppes and deserts have "pumped" people outward when conditions in the steppes are dry. When conditions grow moist again, people remain on the steppes or pull back from surrounding areas (Fagan 2008, 46–47).

Unlike the dynamic steppes and deserts, the more stable civilizations in the river valleys of the Middle East were not cradles of prophets, visions, and revealed religions. Why?

The climate of the Egypt and Mesopotamia was arid. Even in spring, there were no vast grasslands in which domestic animals could graze. Moreover, temperatures rarely dipped below freezing in the winter. The hallucinogenic fungus could not thrive in such conditions.

Unlike settled farmers, pastoral nomads had better opportunities to collect a large supply of the hallucinogen. At the right moment in spring, the owner of a herd of grazing mammals might observe a change in their milk that would indicate the availability of *Claviceps paspali*. The spring milk could serve to enlarge the supply of the drug.

A Time of Drought, 2200–400 B.C.E.

Beginning around 2200 B.C.E., when conditions became markedly drier in the Middle East, the northern part of the Akkadian Empire in Mesopotamia collapsed. The record of changing Dead Sea levels shows that the region remained arid up to c. 400 B.C.E. (Enzel et al. 2003: Burroughs 2005, 251).

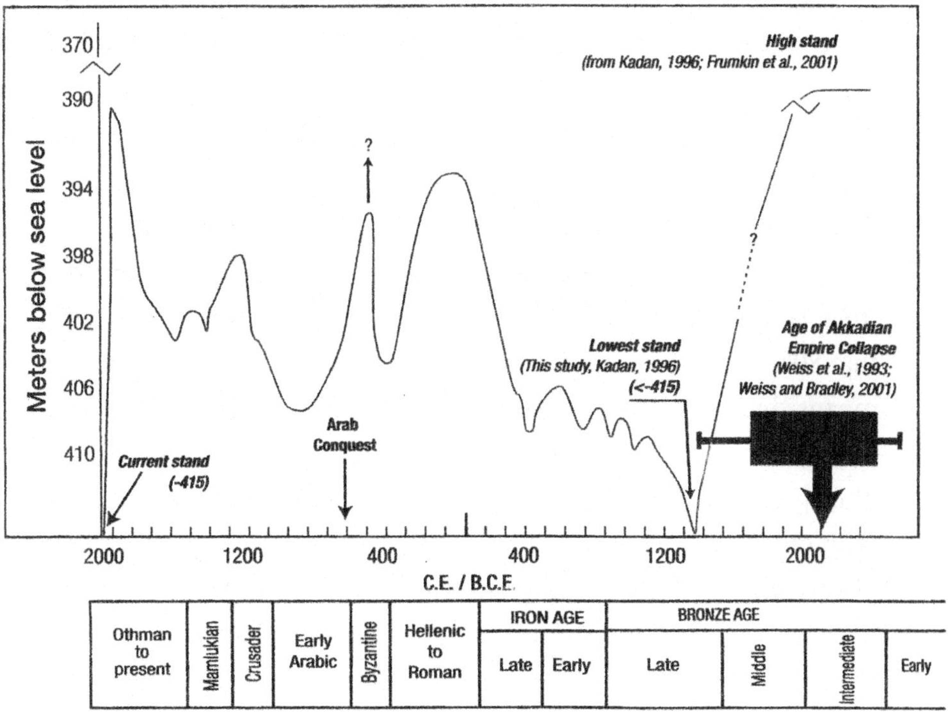

Figure 15. Dead Sea levels, 2000 B.C.E. to 2000 C.E.

The period of drought "pumped" many Indo-Europeans out of Anatolia. The Medes and Persians, who invaded Iran around 1800 B.C.E. used chariots to conquer land from the Zagros Mountains in the west to Afghanistan in the east, and from the Indian Ocean in the south to Central Asia in the north. The Hittites, who were Indo-European inhabitants of eastern Anatolia were using chariots in the late seventeenth century B.C.E. The Armenians in eastern Anatolia were also Indo-Europeans. Chariots were mainly useful in battles fought on large flat plains, especially plains with grass for horse fodder. They were of little use in Greece, which was mainly forested and mountainous.

Although, by the second millennium B.C.E., some men in the Middle East could ride horseback, the Indo-Europeans lacked the necessary equipment and skill to control a horse on the battlefield. They had neither saddles nor stirrups, only reins and a bit. When threatened, horses naturally tended to flee. As herd animals, they were more comfortable with other horses, as when pulling a wheeled vehicle as a team. Only by long conditioning could a lone horse learn to obey a rider reliably amid the noise and terror of battle.

The Indo-Europeans conquered most of Europe and established their languages in the territory. Geneticists have found, however, that 80% of the genes of Europeans are from Paleolithic stock. This means that the Indo-Europeans did not annihilate the indigenous population and repopulate the continent from their own loins. The spread of Indo-European languages, social organization, and religious ideas was mainly a cultural conquest based on the spread of agriculture. This was probably the case in the Middle East as well.

The Middle East had fewer grassy plains than the Eurasian steppe, the homeland of horses. Thus, the cost of feeding a horse was higher. Nevertheless, by the seventeenth century B.C.E., chariot-riding troops became the most important unit in Middle Eastern armies and remained so until the fourth century B.C.E.

The armies of the Canaanite Hyksos people were equipped with chariots and the more powerful composite bow. They began to move into Lower Egypt in the seventeenth century B.C.E. and built a town called Avaria on the shore of the Delta. The Hyksos ruled Lower Egypt from 1674 to 1548 B.C.E., when a native Egyptian dynasty, having adopted the new technologies, expelled the Hyksos and did its best to erase all trace of them.

Another essential element in the new military technology was metal. Beginning in 3000 B.C.E., bronze objects (made from a mixture of copper blended with tin or arsenic) began to be produced, especially in the Anatolian highlands where both copper and tin were available. Mesopotamia and Egypt lacked these ingredients and had to import them. In the Middle Bronze Age, 2000–1600 B.C.E., trade in the ingredients of bronze was active in the Mediterranean Sea.

The Introduction of Iron Tools and Weapons

The Indo-European Hittites in Anatolia and the peoples of the Caucasus produced iron objects in the fourteenth century B.C.E. Iron became dominant in the Middle East c. 1200 B.C.E., supplanting bronze c. 1000 B.C.E. Iron was harder, had a higher melting point, and was cheaper to produced from the abundant ore available. Unfortunately, this contributed to an arms race.

The year 1200 B.C.E. (more or less) also marked both the end of Minoan and Hittite Civilizations. This was a time of severe drought. The international political system collapsed as invading "Sea People" destroyed at least 47 major sites in Greece, Crete, Anatolia, Cyprus and Syria-Levant. Only Mesopotamia was undisturbed. The Egyptians fought off the attackers but were forced to pull back from Syria-Palestine in 605 B.C.E. Their withdrawal liberated the Israelites and enabled them to found two small independent states.

The Sea People are now thought to have come to the land of Canaan from the Aegean, probably Crete, where Greeks were then living alongside indigenous Cretans. The Sea People were the ancestors of the Philistines, who settled on the southern coast of Palestine and gave the country its name.

Camels and Cavalry

The year 1200 B.C.E. also saw the use of camels in the caravan trade between Southern Arabia and Syria. Goods shipped through the Red Sea and the Gulf of Aqaba had to travel by land through desert territory to reach Syria. The drying of the climate reduced the amount of fodder in the deserts and therefore necessitated the use of camels. In the eighth century B.C.E. camels were bred on a large scale for commercial purposes. This had important consequences for the history of religion.

The network of camel caravan routes established in the Fertile Crescent, Anatolia and later across North Africa linked the fertile river valleys and coastal littorals which were separated by wide deserts. Both goods and ideas traveled on the new caravan routes. Psychoactive plants were distributed over the network. Zoroastrianism ideas spread from Persia in all directions. (The original Persian name for Zoroaster was Zarathu-shtra, which indicates that the prophet owned at least one camel, or *shoter.)* The network of caravan routes served as an infrastructure of a larger society.

The sea lanes carried fleets of ships. In the Mediterranean the Phoenicians were the most active, establishing colonies in North Africa, notably Carthage (Tunis).

New iron tack (equipment) for controlling horses was more effective. The Assyrians were the first to train the horse enough to be ridden, alone and in groups, on the terrifying battlefield. According to Robert Drews trained cavalry did not appear anywhere until c. 800 B.C.E., but as early as 750–500 B.C.E., mounted riders greatly unsettled the Middle East (Drews 2004, 138–146). Herodotus reported that the Persians had superior cavalry (*Histories* 6. 94–140).

Mastering a horse may have had profound effects on the minds of Persian, Greek and other men and contributed to their political and religious ideas. From this time to the Industrial Revolution all upper-class males in Western civilization rode horseback. The horse is a status symbol even today.

To ride a horse requires understanding of equine behavior and at the same time a steady will to dominate the animal. A horse cannot be reasoned with: it must be conditioned, that is, rewarded or not rewarded according to its performance. The sort of man who can dominate a horse is likely to be resistant to the domination of others. Only upper-class females, if any, rode horseback. In Minoan Crete, where women appeared dominant in the religion, there were no horsemen; indeed, there were no horses on Crete until the Mycenaean Greeks arrived, c. 1420.

Invention of the Alphabet

Around 1050 B.C.E. the Phoenicians invented the first alphabet. Since their language was Semitic, the words were based on three-consonant roots. There were two long vowels; short vowels were merely implied. The Greeks, who also distinguished themselves as marine traders, added vowels to the Phoenician alphabet. The subsequent alphabets devised in Europe and the Middle East were all derived from the Phoenician-Greek original. These alphabets could be learned quickly, even by small children. This invention made possible the recording of religious traditions and innovations which previously had been transmitted only orally.

Conclusion

This overview of the history of religion in the Middle East from 2200 to 400 B.C.E. has covered religious changes brought about by drought, the military use of the horse and wheel, the commercial use of camels, the invention of the alphabet, and the use of new psychoactive substances.

Male dominance in religion increased. Yahweh became a god of war, as did other male gods. Countries formerly protected by water (e.g. Minoan Crete) and by distance itself were no longer secure. Thus military considerations strongly influenced politics and religion.

The increased violence and suffering may have provoked people to think about evil at a deeper level. Some gave less attention to symbolic animals, to the starry sky, to tribal ancestors, and to deities associated with natural places and the weather. These deities provided neither help nor explanations in times of trouble. People searched for a narrative that explained how life could go so wrong and gave them the hope of a happy ending.

The answer was to be the moralization of religion, which will be discussed in Chapters Eight and Nine.

Chapter Five and Six are devoted to the Minoan religion, the only humanized and female-dominant religion of the period, at more length. Why did Minoan civilization collapse? Why did its religion fail to compete with Zoroastrianism, Judaism, and Christianity?

References

Anthony, David W. 2007. *The Horse, the Wheel, and Language: How Bronze-Age Riders from the European Steppes Shaped the Modern World.* Princeton: Princeton University Press.

Boyce, Mary, ed. and transl. 1984. *Textual Sources for the Study of Zoroastrianism.* Chicago: University of Chicago Press.

Brereton, Joel P. 2005. "Soma." In *Encyclopedia of Religion*, edited by Lindsay Jones, Mircea Eliade, and Charles J. Adams. 2nd ed., vol. 12, 8521–8522. Detroit: Macmillan Reference USA.

Brown, H. B. 1916. "Life History and Poisonous Properties of *Claviceps Paspali*," *Journal of Agricultural Research* 7(9): 401–406.

Burroughs, William J. 2005. *Climate Change in Prehistory: The End of the Reign of Chaos*. Cambridge: Cambridge University Press.

Drews, Robert. 2004. *Early Riders: The Beginnings of Mounted Warfare in Asia and Europe*. New York: Routledge.

Enzel, Yehouda, et al. 2003. "Late Holocene Climates of the Near East Deduced from Dead Sea Level Variations and Modern Regional Winter Rainfall." *Quaternary Research* 60(3): 263–273.

Fagan, Brian. 2009. *The Great Warming: Climate Change and the Rise and Fall of Civilizations*. New York; Bloomsbury Publishing USA.

Falk, Harry. 1989. "Soma I and II." *Bulletin of the School of Oriental and African Studies* 52: 77–90.

Gnoli, Gherardo. 2005. "Haoma." *Encyclopedia of Religion*, vol. 6, 3775–3776.

Greene, Mott T. 1992. *Natural Knowledge in Preclassical Antiquity*. Baltimore: Johns Hopkins.

Herodotus. 440 B.C.E. *History of the Greco-Persian War*.

Hyland, Ann. 2003. *The Horse in the Ancient World*. Westport, Conn.: Praeger.

Lilley, Harvey. 2007. "The Wave that Destroyed Atlantis." BBC Timewatch, April 20.

Lincoln, Bruce. 2005. "Indo-European Religions." *Encyclopedia of Religion,* vol. 7, 4452–4455.

Matthee, Rudi. 2005. *The Pursuit of Pleasure: Drugs and Stimulants in Iranian History, 1500–1900.* Princeton: Princeton University Press.

McGovern, Patrick E. 2003. *Ancient Wine: The Search for the Origins of Viniculture.* Princeton: Princeton University Press.

Pringle, Heather. 2012. "New Method Puts Elusive Indo-European Homeland in Anatolia." *Science* 337 (6097): 902. August 24.

"Proto-Indo-Europeans." Wikipedia.

Renfrew, Colin. 1998. "All the King's Horses: Assessing Cognitive Maps in Later Prehistoric Europe." In *Creativity in Human Evolution and Prehistory,* edited by Steven Mithen, 260–284. New York: Routledge.

Settegast, Mary. 2005. *When Zarathustra Spoke: The Reformation of Neolithic Culture and Religion.* Costa Mesa, Calif.: Mazda Publications.

Snell, Daniel C., ed. 2005. *A Companion to the Ancient Near East.* Oxford: Blackwell.

Wade, Nicholas. 2012. "Family Tree of Languages Has Roots in Anatolia, Biologists Say." *New York Times.* August 23.

Watkins, Calvert. 1978. "Let Us Now Praise Famous Grains." *Proceedings of the American Philosophical Society* 122(1): 9–17.

Chapter Five

The Phaistos Disk

Archaeologist Luigi Pernier discovered the Phaistos Disk in the ruins of the first palace at Phaistos, Crete, which had been destroyed by a severe earthquake. The baked clay disk, 16.5 cm in diameter and inscribed in a unique writing system, has never been deciphered. Some experts have argued that no attempt to decipher the Phaistos Disk is worthwhile because no appropriate "Rosetta Stone" has yet been discovered.

In a 1976 essay, Leon Pomerance argued that the Phaistos Disk was a farmer's almanac or calendar. He convincingly identified two celestial symbols on the Disk: the eagle as the constellation Aquila and the seven dots inside a circle as the Pleiades. But Pomerance arbitrarily assigned the date 2000 B.C.E. as the year of observation represented on the calendar, and he had no computer model of the changing night sky over the course of a year in the remote past.

In 1996 Göran Henriksson and Mary Blomberg suggested that the Minoans had observatories in the peak sanctuaries of Petsophas and Graostalos. Henriksson and Blomberg considered the orientation of the heliacal rising of Arcturus as a reference point for regulating a lunar-solar calendar. So what was that calendar?

A further contribution to the calendar theory came in 2011. On the basis of evidence from Knossos, Henriksson and Blomberg concluded that the Minoans had a solar calendar. The year began with the autumn equinox.

It may be that the main obstacle to decipherment has been the assumption that the signs on the Disk can only be understood by discovering the syllables or words that they supposedly represent. But a pictogram can convey a meaning directly, without sounds, to those familiar with ancient symbols and mythology.

Theories of the Origin of the Greek Constellations.

Michael Ovenden argued that the constellations recognized by the Greeks had been invented in 2800 B.C.E. ± 800 years. He designated the most likely place of invention as latitude 36.5° N by longitude 26.3° E. As to the identity of the inventors of the constellations Ovenden said, "I would like to put forward the claim of the Minoans, based in Crete, who were in the Mediterranean in strength by the beginning of third millennium [B.C.E.]" (Ovenden 1966:15–16).

John Pratt, in discussing the scientific dating of the origin of the constellations, selected the year 2600 B.C.E. ± 800 years. The latter estimate would place Minoan Crete in contention for the honor.

Bradley Schaefer argued that the Greek constellations, as catalogued by Ptolemy of Alexandria in the second-century B.C.E. *Almagest*, originated in Mesopotamia between 1300 and 1000 B.C.E. Taking precession into account, Schaefer argued that the Mesopotamian constellations would have been visible near or at northern latitude 33–36.

But latitude 36 crosses the far north of Mesopotamia. Schaefer gave no likely longitude to justify his choice of Mesopotamia. Nor did he explain why the date of origin of the Mesopotamian constellations was later than the scientifically estimated mean date (2600–2900 B.C.E. ± 800 years). He also did not account for eighteen Greek constellations that had no equivalent in the Mesopotamia (Schaefer 2006).

The palace at Phaistos was in south-central Crete at Latitude 35° N and longitude 25° E. This was quite close to the location specified by Michael Ovenden for the invention of the constellations. The palace commanded a view of the sea to the west, the twin peaks of Mount Ida due north, and the fertile Messara Plain to the east (Willetts 1977, 28–29; Fitton 2002, 6). An observer in Phaistos could use the space between the twin peaks of Mount Ida ("The Mount of the Goddess") as a horizon reference point for due north while sighting the movements of the sun, moon, stars and planets.

The Bronze Age Minoans left us no records of their astronomical observations. They could not refer to written records to predict the changing positions of planets. Consequently they were probably *naïve observers.* They could not have created a calendar which included planetary observations that would be applicable over a long period of time. But they could write a descriptive almanac for the solar year with short-term predictive value.

Dating the Phaistos Disk

The dating of the Category 7 (most severe) volcanic eruption of nearby Mt. Santorini has been confirmed by recent dendrochronological studies which concluded that a likely time of climatic disturbance was in the range of 1627–1600 B.C.E. All the old palaces in Crete were destroyed by an earthquake in this period. Accordingly this decipherment of the Phaistos Disk was based on the median date, 1613 B.C.E. (Friedrich 2006, Manning 2006). Since the Disk was found in the ruins of the Phaistos palace, it was probably in use in that year. A second computer run of the data for 1650 gave results only about an hour different.

The dating of the Phaistos Disk is only an educated guess. All we can be reasonably sure of is that the Disk was made sometime in the seventeenth century B.C.E. before the destruction of the Phaistos palace. However, the proof was in testing the meaning of every sign on the Disk against its projected seasonal and celestial background.

Methodology

The computer program used here was *Your Sky*, prepared by John Walker, founder of Autodesk, and posted on the Internet in 2003. Its virtual telescope was set for 35° N by 25° E, close to the ruins of Phaistos. The dates tested were 1613 and 1650 B.C.E. The significant positions of stars and planets were 1) near the eastern or western horizon at dawn, 2) the peak (culmination) and 3) near the eastern or western horizon at sunset.

The hypothesized interpretations of the signs on the Disk were tested in two ways. The first was to match the signs with the seasonal sequence of events in agriculture, based on the climate of Crete and the changing condition of the plants and animals found there. The other was to match the signs with contemporary events in the sky, specifically, the rise, peak (culmination), and setting of constellations, planets, the sun, and the moon, as shown in computer reconstructions.

The group of stars now called Leo was represented on the Disk by an olive branch and did not include the head of the zodiacal Lion. According to Greek mythology, Herakles killed the Nemean Lion and used its hollowed out skull as a helmet. The "olive branch" represents the remains of the dead lion.

The cluster now called Scorpius was represented on the Disk by a grapevine, bare in winter and leafy in summer. Inspired by the Minoan fresco known as the "Prince of Lilies," I hypothesized that the Cretans saw Scorpius inverted. It was an outline of the god Dionysos and therefore connected with grapevines. These two exceptions do not conflict with Ovenden's theory, which does not specify the exact form of all the constellations invented in 2800 ± 800 years.

When a symbol on the Disk matched the date of a known agricultural or celestial event, that result was taken as a positive verification. Equally important was the *absence* of such symbols at times in the year when no such events normally occurred. The correlations between agricultural and celestial events were usually significant, suggesting that the motivation for creating the Phaistos Disk was the need to schedule agricultural events with accuracy.

The correlations between agricultural and celestial events were so close that I began to wonder if the Phaistos Disk might be a forgery. However, the Disk was discovered in 1908, at least sixty years before the invention of computers and the necessary computer software to recreate the sky over Crete in the seventeenth century B.C.E.

The Phaistos Disk appears to be a 360-day Minoan calendar produced by local observations of the night sky. Its signs can be shown to be pictograms which, with the use of the computer, can be linked to celestial correlates (or analogues). They can be interpreted with reference to Cretan agriculture and Greek myths.

It was not uncommon for ancient peoples to time their seasonal activities to the regular risings and settings of constellations. The ancient Greeks and Romans used changes in the rising, peak and setting of stars and planets to determine the correct timing for farm work (Hannah 2005, 20–27). Archaeoastronomers have shown that many ancient peoples have made surprisingly accurate observations using simple methods (Aveni, 2000, 56, 256–257).

Let us suppose that the climate of Crete today is much the same as the climate in the Late Bronze Age. The months of June, July, and August are hot. In September the weather begins to cool, and October is comfortable. The rainy season starts in late October and lasts until March or April. However, there is a week in January when the weather is fair and the winds die down. Winter is mild. Wild flowers bloom in April and there is no rain after May 10. In May the weather is ideal for sailing, clear and warm, and the sea is calm ("Weather in Crete," explorecrete.com/nature/crete-weather.html).

In one respect the climate of Crete in the seventeenth century B.C.E. may have been different. Hesiod, a Greek writer of c. 700 B.C.E., reported rain in Greece in September (Hannah 2005, 28). The climate of Crete is thought to have been wetter in 1613 B.C.E. than today (Fitton 2002, 58). So the planting of crops in September, as suggested in this decipherment, seems plausible.

It seems correct to read the signs on the Disk from the center out, since the maker of a spiral tends to start from the center and wind around it. There is no doubt that the signs were imprinted on the Disk from right to left, that is, clockwise (Taylour and Chadwick 2004, 332). Those who have tried to interpret the Disk from the outside in (counter-clockwise) have all failed.

Evidence of Time-Factored Character

It is hard to recognize the Disk as a calendar because there are only 122 signs on side A and 119 signs on side B: 122 + 119 = 241. However, on both sides of the Disk are small circles containing seven dots inside. The circle itself was counted as one unit among the original 122 and 119 signs. The seven dots inside were counted as an additional seven days each (Black and Green 1992, 161). There are fifteen of these circles on side A: 15 x 7 = 105. There are two of these circles on side B: 2 x 7 = 14.

Adding 122 + 105 for side A = 227.

Adding 119 + 14 for side B = 133.

Adding 227 + 133 = 360.

This coincided exactly with the Egyptian calendar of 360 days, plus five intercalary days. The number 360 divides into 12 months of exactly thirty days each.

In Mitanni glyphic art, seven dots designated the Pleiades. They were common in Neo-Assyrian and Neo-Babylonian inscriptions. But they were not surrounded by a circle. On the Phaistos Disk the circle around 7 dots served both to indicate 8 days and to indicate the time the Pleiades appeared.

But if the Phaistos Disk is a calendar, why is it divided into two parts, one on side A, and one on side B? The key to understanding this is that Mediterranean agriculture has two sowing seasons a year, a sowing of grain in September for harvest around March, and a sowing of quick-maturing crops soon afterwards so that the harvest is completed by the summer solstice, June 21.

Some important agricultural activities continued in the dry season. Cultivated olives and grapes had very deep roots to reach ground water. Other plants like the opium poppy were drought-resistant and, once sprouted, could survive without water for weeks. Consequently the two sides of the Disk portrayed two different planting seasons with continuity over the summer on Side B.

A period of five intercalary days was probably inserted at the end of August, as suggested by a gap at the end of Side B. That time of year was too hot for productive work, but activity could easily continue during the mild weather of the winter solstice. There is no suggestion on the Disk of a winter break like that of our Gregorian calendar on December 31. This decipherment decision is supported by the practice of the Egyptians, who inserted five intercalary days at the end of August (Hannah 2005, 85–89). The calendar year began as the summer's worst heat was subsiding and rains revived plant life. This may have been the case in Minoan Crete as well.

To decipher the Disk, several initial dates were chosen for Side A. The initial date for Side B necessarily followed from the first decision. After some trial and error the first sign on side A was assigned the date September 1, making the last date April 15, and consequently side B began on April 16 and ended on August 26. Five intercalary days were inserted for August 27–31. (See Chart.)

Decipherment of the Phaistos Disk: Side A

Symbol Number	*Dates*	*Symbol Icon*	*Symbol Name and Position of Celestial Analogue*
1	9–1		Rosette (Opium) – Venus and Mercury at 7 a.m.; new moon
2	9–2		Hermes – Mercury rose at 7 a.m.
3	9–3		Ear of grain – Spica (in Virgo) rose at 5 a.m.
4	9–4		Runner – Boötes rose at 5 a.m.
5	9–5		Club – Hercules peaked at 5 p.m.
6	9–6		Palace – Canopus rose at 5 a.m.
7	9–7		Poppy – Venus set at 6 p.m.
8	9–8		Olive branch – Leo peaked at 7 a.m.
9	9–9		Sheepskin – Aries set at 5:30 a.m.
10	9–10		Sheepskin – Aries set at 5:30 a.m.
11	9–11 to 9–18		Eight-day period; Pleiades set at 6 a.m.
12	9–19		Warrior – Mars peaked at 8 a.m.
13	9–20		Rosette – Venus and Mercury rose at dawn.
14	9–21		Hermes – Mercury rose at 7 a.m.
15	9–22		Ear of grain – Spica rose at 4 a.m.
16	9–23		Olive branch – Leo peaked at 7 a.m.

Decipherment of the Phaistos Disk: Side A

Symbol Number	*Dates*	*Symbol Icon*	*Symbol Name and Position of Celestial Analogue*
17	9–24		Grapevine, bare – Scorpius (Dionysos) rose at 8 a.m.
18	9–25		Hammer – Jupiter rose at 4 a.m.
19	9–26		Runner – Boötes rose at 4 a.m.
20	9–27		Club – Hercules rose at 8 a.m.
21	9–28 to 10–5		Eight-day period; Pleiades set at 5 a.m.
22	10–6		Hermes – Mercury and four other planets visible at 8 a.m.
23	10–7 to 10–14		Eight-day period; Pleiades set at 4:30 a.m.
24	10–15		Horn of bull – Taurus set at 5 a.m.
25	10–16		Eagle – Aquila set at 7 p.m.
26	10–17		Grapevine – Scorpius rose at 5:30 a.m.; Virgo and Corona Borealis visible; Saturn and Mars in conjunction; full moon
27	10–18		Cymbal – Saturn and Mars in conjunction at 5:30 a.m.
28	10–19		Migrating birds – Cygnus peaked at 5 p.m.
29	10–20		Dancing woman – Venus in west at 5 p.m.
30	10–21		Sheep – Aries rose at 4 p.m.
31	10–22		Migrating birds – Cygnus peaked at 5 p.m.

Decipherment of the Phaistos Disk: Side A

Symbol Number	*Dates*	*Symbol Icon*	*Symbol Name and Position of Celestial Analogue*
32	10–23		Dove – Columba set in SW at 4 a.m.
33	10–24		Scales – Libra rose at 4 a.m.
34	10–25		Aries – near peak at 7 a.m.
35	10–26 to 11–2		Eight-day period; Pleiades set at 3 a.m.
36	11–3		Warrior – Mars peaked at 7:30 a.m.
37	11–4		Horn of bull – Taurus rose at 5 p.m.
38	11–5		Eagle – Aquila set at 6 p.m.
39	11–6 to 11–13		Eight-day period; Pleiades rose at 5 p.m.
40	11–14		Warrior – Mars peaked at 7 a.m.
41	11–15		Runner – Boötes peaked at 7 a.m.
42	11–16		Goat leg – Capricorn set at 5 p.m.
43	11–17		Migrating birds – Cygnus rose at 7 a.m.
44	11–18		Hammer – Jupiter peaked at 7 a.m.
45	11–19		Ear of grain – Spica in Virgo peaked at 6 a.m.
46	11–20		Ship – Vela set at 6 a.m.
47	11–21		Sheepskin – Aries peaked at 6 a.m.

Decipherment of the Phaistos Disk: Side A

Symbol Number	*Dates*	*Symbol Icon*	*Symbol Name and Position of Celestial Analogue*
48	11–22		Warrior – Mars peaked at 7 a.m.
49	11–23		Horn of bull – Taurus rose at 4 p.m.
50	11–24		Eagle – Aquila rose at 6 a.m.
51	11–25 to 12–2		Eight-day period; Pleiades rose at 3 p.m.
52	12–3		Warrior – Mars peaked at 7 a.m.
53	12–4		Hammer – Jupiter peaked at 7 a.m.
54	12–5		Fish – Pisces peaked at 4 p.m.
55	12–6		Palace – Scorpius, Virgo and Corona Borealis peaked at 7 a.m.
56	12–7		Poppy – Venus rose and Mercury peaked at 9 a.m.
57	12–8		Olive branch – Leo rose at 6 p.m.
58	12–9		Sheepskin – Aries peaked at 5 p.m.
59	12–10		Sheepskin – Aries peaked at 5 p.m.
60	12–11 to 12–18	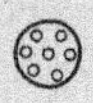	Eight-day period; Pleiades peaked at 7 p.m.
61	12–19		Warrior – Mars peaked at 7 a.m.
62	12–20		Horn of bull – Taurus peaked at 7 p.m.
63	12–21		Eagle – Aquila rose at 4:30 a.m.

Decipherment of the Phaistos Disk: Side A

Symbol Number	*Dates*	*Symbol Icon*	*Symbol Name and Position of Celestial Analogue*
64	12–22 to 12–29		Eight-day period; Pleiades peaked at 7 a.m.
65	12–30		Warrior – Mars peaked at 7 a.m.
66	12–31		Runner – Boötes rose at 8 p.m.
67	1–1		Goat leg – Capricorn rose at 7 a.m.
68	1–2		Migrating bird – Cygnus peaked at 9 a.m.
69	1–3		Hammer – Jupiter peaked at 5 a.m.; conjunction with Saturn
70	1–4		Ear of grain – Spica in Virgo set at 8 a.m.
71	1–5		Ship – Vela rose at 8 a.m.
72	1–6		Sheepskin – Aries peaked at 4 a.m.
73	1–7		Warrior – Mars set at 6 p.m.
74	1–8		Bow – Sagittarius rose at 4 a.m.
75	1–9		Lily – Delphinus peaked at 9 a.m.
76	1–10		Rosette – Mercury and Venus peaked at 9 a.m.
77	1–11		Hammer – Jupiter set at 8 a.m.
78	1–12		Dove – Columba peaked at 7:30 a.m.
79	1–13 to 1–20		Eight-day period; Pleiades peaked at 5 a.m.

Decipherment of the Phaistos Disk: Side A

Symbol Number	*Dates*	*Symbol Icon*	*Symbol Name and Position of Celestial Analogue*
80	1–21		Warrior – Mars rose at 4 p.m.
81	1–22		Pubic triangle – Venus rose in SE at 5 a.m.
82	1–23		Venus legs – Venus rose in SE at 5 a.m.
83	1–24		Pan pipes – Virgo set at 7 a.m.; Capricorn in SE
84	1–25		Runner – Boötes rose at 7 p.m.
85	1–26		Olive branch – Leo rose at 4:30 p.m.
86	1–27		Grapevine, bare – Scorpius peaked at 5 a.m.
87	1–28		Pan pipes – Virgo set at 7 a.m.; Capricorn in SE
88	1–29 to 2–5		Eight-day period; Pleiades at peak at 4:30 p.m.
89	2–6		Warrior – Mars set at 6 p.m.
90	2–7		Olive branch – Leo peaked at 8:30 p.m.
91	2–8		Horn of bull – Taurus set at 8 p.m.
92	2–9		Eagle – Aquila peaked at 7 a.m.
93	2–10		Migrating birds – Cygnus peaked at 8 a.m.
94	2–11		Woman dancing – Venus rose SE at 5 a.m.

Decipherment of the Phaistos Disk: Side A

Symbol Number	*Dates*	*Symbol Icon*	*Symbol Name and Position of Celestial Analogue*
95	2–12 to 2–19		Eight-day period; Pleiades set at 8 p.m.
96	2–20		Warrior – Mars rose at 7:30 a.m.
97	2–21		Wrapped hand – Gemini peaked at 5 p.m.
98	2–22		Outline of Virgo – Virgo rose at 5:30 p.m.
99	2–23		Sheepskin – Aries rose at 7 a.m.
100	2–24 to 3–3		Eight-day period; Pleiades rose at 8 a.m.
101	3–4		Pubic triangle – Venus rose at 5 a.m.
102	3–5		Water – Aquarius rose at 4 a.m.
103	3–6		Sheepskin – Aries at 6 a.m.
104	3–7		Fish – Pisces rose at 6 a.m.
105	3–8		Venus legs – Venus rose at 5:30 a.m.
106	3–9		Carrier – Aquarius rose at 4:30 a.m.
107	3–10 to 3–17		Eight-day period; Pleiades rose at 7 a.m.
108	3–18		Warrior – Mars set at 5:30 p.m.
109	3–19		Bee – Orion set, Jupiter near peak at 7 p.m.

Decipherment of the Phaistos Disk: Side A

Symbol Number	*Dates*	*Symbol Icon*	*Symbol Name and Position of Celestial Analogue*
110	3–20		Dog – Canis Major set at 8 p.m.
111	3–21		Dog – Canis Minor set at 8 p.m.
112	3–22		Pubic triangle – Venus rose at 5 a.m.
113	3–23		Water – Aquarius rose at 5:30 a.m.
114	3–24		Dog – Canis Minor set at 7 p.m.
115	3–25 to 4–1		Eight-day period; Pleiades set at 5 p.m.
116	4–2		Venus legs – Venus rose at 5 a.m.
117	4–3		Beehive – Pleiades rose at 6 a.m.
118	4–4		Migrating birds – Cygnus peaked at 6 a.m.
119	4–5		Runner – Boötes set at 5 a.m.
120	4–6		Club – Hercules set at 8 a.m.
121	4–7 to 4–14		Eight-day period; Pleiades rose at 5 a.m.
122	4–15		Warrior – Mars at peak at 5:30 a.m.

Decipherment of the Phaistos Disk: Side B

Symbol Number	*Dates*	*Symbol Icon*	*Symbol Name and Position of Celestial Analogue*
1	4–16		Pubic triangle – Venus rose at 4:30 a.m.
2	4–17		Water – Aquarius peaked at 5 a.m.
3	4–18		Ship – Puppis and Vela set at 7 p.m.
4	4–19		Hammer – Jupiter peaked at 7 p.m.
5	4–20		Bee – Orion rose at 7 a.m.
6	4–21		Dog – Canis Minor rose at 8 a.m.
7	4–22		Pubic triangle – Venus rose at 5 a.m.
8	4–23		Hammer – Jupiter peaked at 6 p.m.
9	4–24		Olive branch – Leo peaked at 5:30 p.m.
10	4–25		Woman dancing – Venus rose at 5 a.m.
11	4–26		Warrior – Mars rose at 5 a.m.
12	4–27		Pubic triangle – Venus rose at 6 a.m.
13	4–28		Birds migrating – Cygnus peaked at 5 a.m.
14	4–29		Lily – Delphinus peaked at 4 a.m.
15	4–30		Head of ram – Aries rose at 4 a.m.
16	5–1		Lyre – Lyra peaked at 3 a.m.

Decipherment of the Phaistos Disk: Side B

Symbol Number	*Dates*	*Symbol Icon*	*Symbol Name and Position of Celestial Analogue*
17	5-2		Wrapped hand – Gemini rose at 6 a.m.
18	5-3		Pubic triangle – Venus rose at 5 a.m.
19	5-4		Grapevine, leafy – Scorpius rose at 6 p.m.
20	5-5		Dog – Canis Minor rose at 6 a.m.
21	5-6		Root or spun thread – Cancer set at 9 p.m.
22	5-7		Beehive – Pleiades rose at 3 a.m.
23	5-8		Migrating birds – Cygnus peaked at 3 a.m.
24	5-9		Hammer – Jupiter peaked at 6 p.m.
25	5-10		Pubic triangle – Venus rose at 5 a.m.
26	5-11		Pubic triangle – Venus rose at 4 a.m.
27	5-12		Water – Aquarius set at 7 a.m.
28	5-13		Pubic triangle – Venus rose at 4 a.m.
29	5-14		Olive branch – Leo set at 8 p.m.
30	5-15		Migrating birds – Cygnus peaked at 4 a.m.
31	5-16		Pubic triangle – Venus rose at 4 a.m.
32	5-17		Ship – Vela set at 6 p.m.

Decipherment of the Phaistos Disk: Side B

Symbol Number	*Dates*	*Symbol Icon*	*Symbol Name and Position of Celestial Analogue*
33	5–18		Hammer – Jupiter peaked at 6 p.m.
34	5–19		Bee – Orion rose at 5 a.m.
35	5–20		Sheepskin – Aries peaked at 7 a.m.
36	5–21		Wrapped hand – Gemini rose at 5 a.m.
37	5–22		Pubic triangle – Venus rose at 4 a.m.
38	5–23		Grapevine, leafy – Scorpius rose at 5 p.m.
39	5–24		Dog – Canis Minor rose at 6 a.m.
40	5–25		Root or Spun thread – Cancer rose at 6 a.m.
41	5–26		Pubic triangle – Venus rose at 4 a.m.
42	5–27		Water – Aquarius set at 6 a.m.
43	5–28		Dog – Canis Major rose at 7 a.m.
44	5–29		Poppy – Mercury and Venus rose at 4 a.m.
45	5–30		Wrapped hand – Gemini rose at 4 a.m.
46	5–31		Dog – Canis Major rose at 6 a.m.
47	6–1		Wrapped hand – Gemini rose at 4 a.m.
48	6–2		Pubic triangle – Venus rose at 4 a.m.

Decipherment of the Phaistos Disk: Side B

Symbol Number	*Dates*	*Symbol Icon*	*Symbol Name and Position of Celestial Analogue*
49	6–3		Grapevine, leafy – Scorpius rose at 4 p.m.
50	6–4		Dog – Canis Minor rose at 5 a.m.
51	6–5		Runner – Boötes peaked at 6 p.m.
52	6–6		Sheepskin – Aries peaked at 5 a.m.
53	6–7		Lyre – Lyra set at 7 a.m.
54	6–8		Warrior – Mars rose at 4 a.m.
55	6–9		Fish – Pisces peaked at 4 a.m.
56	6–10		Lily – Delphinus set at 6 a.m.
57	6–11		Dove – Columba rose SE at 7 a.m.
58	6–12		Olive branch – Leo set at 7 p.m.
59	6–13		Woman dancing – Venus rose at 4 a.m.
60	6–14		Runner – Boötes set at 6 p.m.
61	6–15		Fish – Pisces peaked at 4 a.m.
62	6–16		Dog – Canis Minor rose at 5 a.m.
63	6–17		Migrating birds – Cygnus set at 7 a.m.
64	6–18		Scales – Libra peaked at 6 p.m.
65	6–19		Knife – Scorpius peaked at 6 p.m.

Decipherment of the Phaistos Disk: Side B

Symbol Number	*Dates*	*Symbol Icon*	*Symbol Name and Position of Celestial Analogue*
66	6–20		Olive branch – Leo rose at 6 a.m.
67	6–21		Jar – Pleiades peaked at 6 a.m.
68	6–22		Beehive – Pleiades peaked at 6 a.m.
69	6–23		Beehive – Pleiades peaked at 6 a.m.
70	6–24		Dog – Canis Major rose at 5 a.m.
71	6–25		Runner – Boötes peaked at 6 p.m.
72	6–26		Rosette – Venus and Mercury rose at 5 a.m.
73	6–27		Ship – Puppis rose in SE at 7 a.m.
74	6–28		Sheepskin – Aries peaked at 4 a.m.
75	6–29		Venus legs – Venus rose at 5 a.m.
76	6–30		Grapevine – Scorpius peaked at 6 p.m.
77	7–1		Horn of bull – Taurus peaked at 5 a.m.
78	7–2		Warrior – Mars rose at 4 a.m.
79	7–3		Olive branch – Leo rose at 5 a.m.
80	7–4		Venus legs – Venus rose at 5 a.m.
81	7–5		Beehive – Pleiades peaked at 5 a.m.

Decipherment of the Phaistos Disk: Side B

Symbol Number	*Dates*	*Symbol Icon*	*Symbol Name and Position of Celestial Analogue*
82	7-6		Pubic triangle – Venus rose at 5 a.m.
83	7-7		Ship – Puppis rose in SE at 6 a.m.
84	7-8		Torn hymen – Virgo set at 7 p.m.; Jupiter passing out of Virgo.
85	7-9		Poppy – Mercury and Venus rose at 6 a.m.
86	7-10		Root or Spun Thread – Cancer rose at 4 a.m.
87	7-11		Migrating birds – Cygnus set at 6 a.m.
88	7-12		Runner – Boötes near peak at 6:30 a.m.
89	7-13		Club – Hercules peaked at 6:30 p.m.
90	7-14		Pubic triangle – Venus rose at 5 a.m.
91	7-15		Axe – at 7 a.m. Taurus, Gemini, and Orion peaked; all 5 planets visible.
92	7-16		Fish – Pisces set at 6 a.m.
93	7-17		Lily – Delphinus peaked at 8 p.m.
94	7-18		Runner – Boötes rose at 7 a.m.
95	7-19		Club – Hercules peaked at 7 p.m.
96	7-20		Pubic triangle containing seeds – Venus rose at 5 a.m.

Decipherment of the Phaistos Disk: Side B

Symbol Number	*Dates*	*Symbol Icon*	*Symbol Name and Position of Celestial Analogue*
97	7–21		Migrating birds – Cygnus set at 5 a.m.
98	7–22		Hammer – Jupiter rose at 7 a.m.
99	7–23	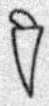	Knife – Scorpius set at 8 p.m.
100	7–24 to 7–31		Eight-day period; Pleiades set at 8 a.m.
101	8–1		Jar – Pleiades set at 9 a.m. and Scorpius set at 8 p.m.
102	8–2		Beehive – Pleiades set at 8 a.m.
103	8–3		Fish – Pisces set at 5 a.m.
104	8–4		Sheepskin – Aries set at 7 a.m.
105	8–5		Ship – Puppis rose at 4 a.m.
106	8–6		Root or Spun thread – Cancer peaked at 7 am.
107	8–7		Man amazed – Boötes rose at 7 a.m.; Gemini and Orion at peak; all 5 planets visible.
108	8–8		Hammer – Jupiter rose at 6 a.m.
109	8–9		Poppy – Mercury near peak at 7 a.m.; Venus visible.
110	8–10		Warrior – Mars peaked at 8 a.m.
111	8–11		Olive branch – Leo peaked at 8 a.m.

Decipherment of the Phaistos Disk: Side B

Symbol Number	*Dates*	*Symbol Icon*	*Symbol Name and Position of Celestial Analogue*
112	8–12		Pubic triangle – Venus rose at 6 a.m. in conjunction with Jupiter
113	8–13		Aquarius rose in SE at 7 a.m.
114	8–14		Sheepskin – Aries set at 7 a.m.
115	8–15		Pubic triangle – Venus rose at 6 a.m.
116	8–16		Venus legs – Venus rose at 6 a.m.
117	8–17		Root or Spun thread – Cancer peaked at 7 a.m.
118	8–18 to 8–25		Eight-day period; Pleiades set at 7 a.m.
119	8–26		Warrior – Mars peaked at 8 a.m.

Findings

Remarkably, eleven of the twelve Greek zodiac constellations—Aquarius, Pisces, Aries, Taurus, Leo, Virgo, Libra, Scorpio, Sagittarius, Capricorn, and Cancer—are symbolized on the Phaistos Disk. These eleven Cretan symbols correspond to the rising, culmination or setting of the constellations they appear to represent.

The missing constellation of Gemini is correlated on the Phaistos Disk with a wrapped hand (suggesting a time for vows). As I suggested in Chapter Two, Gemini may have been the Central Woman. The Minoans may have tabooed the representation of Her. Instead, Her days were occasions on which to make vows.

The eleven zodiac constellations found on the Phaistos Disk were not arranged in a circle divided into equal parts of 30° each. In that sense, it cannot be said that the Minoans invented the zodiac.

In addition, five other important non-zodiac Greek constellations—Orion, Hercules, Cygnus, Lyra, and Argo Navis—mentioned in Ptolemy's *Almagest* appear to match symbols on the Phaistos Disk.

Constellations which appeared in the *Almagest* but *not* on the Phaistos Disk were Ursa Major, Ursa Minor, and Gemini. These constellations may be of a more northern Indo-European origin (the Greeks were Indo-Europeans).

The bright star Arcturus was mentioned in the *Almagest,* but not its constellation Boötes, the Bear herdsman, who appears on the Phaistos Disk. The presence of Boötes and absence of the Bears on the Disk may reflect the fact that the latitude of Phaistos is about three degrees south of Athens. In Crete, Arcturus in Boötes was more prominent than the Bears.

The constellation Delphinus, which appears on the Disk but not in the *Almagest,* was recognized by the Greeks as early as the fifth century B.C.E. It may have originated in Crete.

Aquila, which appears on the Disk but not in the *Almagest,* was the eagle of Zeus in Greek mythology. In some myths, Zeus was born in Crete. In the Rig Veda, an eagle bore the *soma* juice (a hallucinogen) to India.

Of the five planets known to the ancients Mercury, Venus, Mars, and Jupiter are represented on the Disk. The missing planet, Saturn, was in a thirty-year orbit around the sun and therefore appeared nearly stationary from the perspective of an earthly observer.

Four symbols on the Disk represent plants. Three of them were cultivated for food: a cereal (wheat?), the grapevine, and the olive. The fourth is the poppy, the sap of which contains opium.

But that is not all. The Phaistos Disk almanac probably influenced the timing of religious rituals such as the advent of spring, the sacrifice of the first fruits of an important plant, the sacred wedding of a god and goddess, the sacrifice of a sacred bull, and the mid-winter festival.

Interpretation of Symbols

While there are no certain connections between Greek culture and Mycenaean culture, and between Mycenaean culture and Minoan culture, scholars have suggested possible connections among the three. For this reason, the proposed interpretation of the Phaistos Disk refers to Greek mythology.

The Rosette. The appearance of the rosette at the center of Side A suggests opium. The rosette symbol was found with opium seed capsules and poppies in the artifacts of the cults of Inanna and Ishtar in Mesopotamia, Astarte in the Levant, and Demeter in Greece. The rosette resembles the crown of the unripe poppy seed capsule, which contains the opium. It may contain four to eighteen septa, depending on elevation. Six septa are usual in the highlands of Asia Minor, so the eight-septa shown on the Disk rosette would be expected at Phaistos, which was near sea level.

The decipherment of Linear B writing on Minoan tablets firmly established the cultivation of opium in Minoan Crete. According to Karl Kerenyi,

> The clay tablets that have been deciphered testify to the fact that poppies were widely cultivated both in Crete and in Pylos in the Late Minoan period. The use of the poppy head [crown of the poppy seed capsule] as an ideogram in these account books leaves no room for doubt. The yield of poppies mentioned is so enormous that students long suspected that the figures referred to grain rather than poppies (Kerenyi 1976: 23–25).

There was an eight-septa rosette design on the ceiling in the palace of Knossos, Crete. At a small sanctuary in Gazi, a village near Heraklion, the figure of a female with three opium seed capsules stuck by pins in her head was unearthed. Her eyelids were shut and her mouth slightly open, suggesting she had been ingesting or smoking opium (Goodison and Morris 1998, 122).

The opium poppy needs a lot of sun—twelve hours a day during its 40–60 day growth cycle. Once planted in moist conditions it needs no further watering, fertilizing, or other attention. From the time of sowing to the end of harvest in Turkey today is about 73 days.

The rosette is sign 1 on Side A, right in the center of the Phaistos Disk, suggesting importance. It recurs as sign 13 and again as sign 76 (September 1 and 20, and January 10). On both September 1 and 20 the planets Mercury (Hermes) and Venus (Aphrodite) rose at dawn in the east. Venus was associated with opium in Mesopotamia; Hermes, in the Greek Hymn to Demeter. Sign 76 (January 10) may indicate the end of opium processing. Venus and Mercury peaked (culminated) in the sky at 9 a.m.

The rosette on Side B is number 72 (June 26). This appears to be the end of the harvest of the poppies sown in mid-April. After the sprouting of the seeds during the spring rains no irrigation would have been required. At this point Mercury and Venus rose at 5 a.m.

Hermes. Immediately after the first two rosettes on Side A is the profile of a man with 8 mark on his cheek. The 8 mark stood for Hermes (Mercury), the messenger between the worlds of the living and the dead. It represented the mating of two snakes (in myth, Zeus and Hera). This sign was attached to the staff of Hermes, first called the *kerykeion*. Later it was called the *caduceus*, a staff with two wings added to the top and multiple snake windings. The sign of Hermes, which had little to do with medicine, became confused with the rod of Aesculapius and was adopted as a symbol of the medical profession, especially in the United States (Friedlander 1992). It is still the symbol of a physician who, like Hermes, escorts human beings from life to death, but alas, not the reverse.

It was Hermes who brought Persephone back from Hades to her mother, Demeter, on earth. Hermes was from Kyllene, otherwise known as Mekone, the "poppy town" near Corinth (Merlin 1984, 210–211). Hence he is logically connected with the rosette, emblem of opium. Furthermore, consulting the sky for the dates September 2 and 21, one sees that the planet Mercury (Hermes) rose at 7 a.m.

Opium poppy. The sign of a flower on top of a long upright stalk may be an opium poppy. It occurred on May 29, July 9, August 9, September 7, and December 7. It is unclear whether it referred to events in poppy cultivation or occasions for opium use. All poppy signs were correlated with the rise or peak of Mercury and/or Venus.

Ear of Grain. Near to the rosette center of Side A is a symbol that appears to be an ear of grain (Signs 3 and 15, September 3 and 22). On September 3 the bright star Spica rose at 5 a.m. and at 4 a.m. on September 22. This star represents an ear of grain in the hand of the constellation Virgo. Signs 3 and 15 may be planting dates for wheat or barley.

The ear of grain as the star Spica peaked on November 19 and January 4. It peaked at 6:00 a.m. on November 19, and set at 8 a.m. on January 4. The outline of Virgo on February 22 coincided with the rise of Virgo at 5 p.m.

Olives. There were two other important crops grown on Crete: olives and grapes. The leaves of the olive tree, *Olea europaea,* are arranged opposite each other on the stem, which is a way of identifying the sign on the Disk.

Olive trees flower in May and are thinned two weeks after full bloom. The olive fruit needs six to eight months to mature. Olives are harvested from the beginning of November until spring.

The olive branch sign appears eleven times on the Disk. Every appearance was correlated with one of the three significant positions of the constellation now called Leo, excluding his head. The torso of Leo, shaped like an olive branch, is an accurate celestial analogue, including a slight leftward bend of the top of the branch.

In Greek mythology, as mentioned above, Herakles attacked the Nemean Lion with a club made of wild olive wood. The lion survived, so Herakles had to strangle him. He took the hollowed-out cranium of the dead lion to use as a helmet.

Grapevine. The cultivation of the grapevine in Crete began by 2500 B.C.E. Unlike olive trees, grapevines are deciduous and dormant in fall and winter. Archaeologists have found evidence of large-scale retsina wine production in 1700 B.C.E. in the Amari Valley, which was under the control of the palace at Phaistos (McGovern 2003: 247–265).

On Side B, the upright Y *with leaves* seem to be a grapevine sign, the vertical support for the vine. A leafy Y appeared on May 4, June 3, and June 30. A bare Y represented September 24, October 17, and January 27. The last three signs appeared when the vine was dormant.

The Y sign, both bare and leafy, had a celestial analogue: the constellation now called Scorpius. What did the Minoans make of this group of stars?

As a first step, let us examine a male figure from a mural in the palace of Knossos, as reconstructed by an artist employed by Sir Arthur Evans. Evans identified him as Minos, a priest-king. Archaeologists call him the "Prince of Lilies."

Now let us compare the "Prince of Lilies" with the constellation of Scorpius, inverted. Next redraw the constellation to match the figure of the "Prince of Lilies." His left arm extends backward, with the star delta-Ophiuchus as his left hand. His right arm is bent, with the hand on his chest. His right leg extends forward. His midsection is a pelvic triangle, from which is extended a line suggesting an erect penis.

Lily. Observe the bank of Madonna lilies *behind* the figure of the "Prince of Lilies." The lily's tripartite construction suggested the male genitalia. According to modern astrologers, each constellation in the Zodiac is connected with some part of the human body, and the genitalia are connected with the constellation Scorpius.

The lily symbol appears on the Disk on April 29, June 10, July 17, and January 9. Its look-alike analogue in the sky, is Delphinos, the dolphin. Delphinus is *behind* Scorpius-inverted. The first three dates of lily signs fall into the blooming period of the Madonna lily, spring to midsummer. The fourth lily sign for January 9 was the date on which Delphinus was at its peak at 9 a.m. This may have been the time of the mid-winter festival.

Knife-blade. Sign 99 (June 19 and July 23), might be a knife blade suitable for grape harvesting. The first date might have the sacrifice of first fruits of this precious crop. It was close to the summer solstice. The second knife sign might have signaled grape harvest time. On both dates the constellation Scorpius was at its peak.

Then why the appearance of the bare Y sign on September 24, October 17 and January 27? On September 24 Scorpius rose at 8 a.m. On January 27 it peaked at 5 a.m. But October 17 was a date of great significance for watchers of the night sky. At 5:30 a.m. Scorpius (Dionysos) appeared in the east. Saturn and Mars were in conjunction. There was a full moon. Next to Dionysos was Libra, the scales, symbol of balance. Next to Libra was Virgo. Due north of the scales was the constellation Corona Borealis, containing a U of seven bright stars.

According to a Greek myth, Dionysos married Ariadne, princess of Crete and gave her a gold wedding crown (the Corona Borealis). This may be the Cretan version of the sacred marriage between god and goddess, which was found in Mesopotamia earlier and in Greece later.

There are two other mythical assertions about Dionysos which the information on the Disk serves to explain. One is that Dionysos was twice-born. The vine sign appeared on the Disk on May 4, when Scorpius rose at 6 p.m. and October 17, when Scorpius rose at 5:30 a.m.

The second story is that the mother of Dionysos, Semele (or Persephone), carried him only six months, when she died from a thunderbolt thrown by Zeus. For the next three months, Zeus, the father, carried the fetus in his thigh to full term. (The Athenians said Semele carried Dionysos seven months, but they were using a lunar calendar.)

From January 28 to May 3 in 1613 B.C.E., for three months and five days, no grapevine appeared on the Disk. The Zeus sign was also absent in this period. The period may correspond to the supposed three months in which Zeus carried Dionysos in his thigh.

Cancer. The inverse Y sign is that of the present constellation of Cancer the Crab. Without exception it coincided with the rise, setting, or peak of that constellation. The sign may have represented either a root or a thread spun by twisting two fibers.

Originally the crab may have represented a Y-shaped distaff, from which a woman draws two fibers and twists them to make a thread, the first step in spinning. This constellation was next to Gemini, which I have suggested was the Central Woman. This would account for the Greek myths of spinning goddesses, notably Athena, Aphrodite, and the Three Fates. Such figures are common in folklore from all over Europe. The Central Woman with her distaff may be Neolithic in origin. The nearby constellation of Canis Minor, with the bright star Procyon may represent her drop spindle.

Wrapped hand. A zodiac sign not cited so far is Gemini, the Twins. On the Disk a wrapped right hand appeared on February 21, May 2, May 30 and June 1, each time coinciding with a significant position of Gemini. This custom of wrapping one's right hand before shaking hands on a deal is found today in the Middle East. It is still customary when swearing an oath in Western courts to raise one's right hand, palm forward, as in the sign.

There is no trace of a pair of male twins in the mythology and religion of Minoan Crete. The nature of the oath signified, and the god or goddess to whom it was made, is unclear.

Apiculture, the care of honeybees, was practiced in Crete by the Late Bronze Age. It was mentioned in Linear B inscriptions from Crete. Honey was fermented to make mead and was offered to the gods (Fitton 2002, 12).

Beekeeping was also related to celestial phenomena. The Pleiades, a group of seven stars in the constellation of Taurus, were frequently cited by Hesiod, the Greek writer on agriculture, as a sign by which to time agricultural operations. The constellation of Orion and the planet Jupiter (Zeus) were also associated with bees. Orion was born in a town called Hyrai, a form of *hyron*, said to be the Cretan word for a swarm of bees or beehive. Bees in Crete were supposed to have fed Cretan Zeus as a baby.

Bee. Minoan apiculture was revealed on the Disk by the presence of a bee on March 19, April 20, and May 19. That was when the flowers were in bloom, and the bees were beginning to collect nectar. On March 19, near the spring equinox, the Pleiades rose at dawn, Orion set at 7 p.m., and Jupiter was near its peak. The bee symbols on April 20 and May 19 coincided with the rising at dawn of the constellation Orion.

Beehive. The beehive symbol appeared on the Disk on April 3 and May 7 with the rising of the Pleiades in early morning. It appeared next on June 22, June 23, and July 5, when the Pleiades were at their peak at dawn. It last appeared on August 2, when the Pleiades set at 8 a.m. The beehive sign probably signaled the time for removing honey from the hives and cleaning them. It may have signaled the time to pour honey libations for the gods.

Jar. The jar sign appeared on Side B in two places: Symbol 67 (June 21) and Symbol 101 (August 1), in both cases preceding a beehive. It could either have been a honey jar or a wine jar. The celestial analogue of the jar was the Pleiades. The first jar appeared on June 21, the summer solstice. It may have signaled the opening of wine jugs for a festival. When it appeared on August 1 it could have signaled a festival to celebrate the end of the grape harvest. On that day both Scorpius (grapevine correlate) and the Pleiades (honeycomb correlate) set in the west.

There were no apiculture signs during the fall and winter when the bees were hibernating. This was a negative confirmation of the decipherment.

The woman with the long hair flying loose and a long skirt. This sign appeared to be a woman dancing. She appeared on February 11, on April 25, June 13, and October 20. This image was correlated with the presence of the planet Venus (Aphrodite). These may have been days of women's rituals. The occurrence of this sign on February 11, followed by an unspecified eight-day period, may have marked the Cretan celebration of the beginning of spring and the opening of the wine jars half buried in the ground. By this time spring in the Mediterranean area was well under way. In Athens this was the time of the festival of Anthesteria, lasting three days in late February or early March. It was dedicated to Dionysos and Hermes. At this time the wine produced in the preceding year was considered ready to drink and the party season began.

Sideways V. The V turned sideways suggested a flock of migrating birds in flight. Hesiod used the appearance of migrating cranes, either going north toward Europe in the spring, or going south to Africa in the fall, as signs for undertaking agricultural operations (Hannah 2005, 20–21). The sideways V was always correlated with the dawn, peak and evening positions of the constellation Cygnus, the Swan.

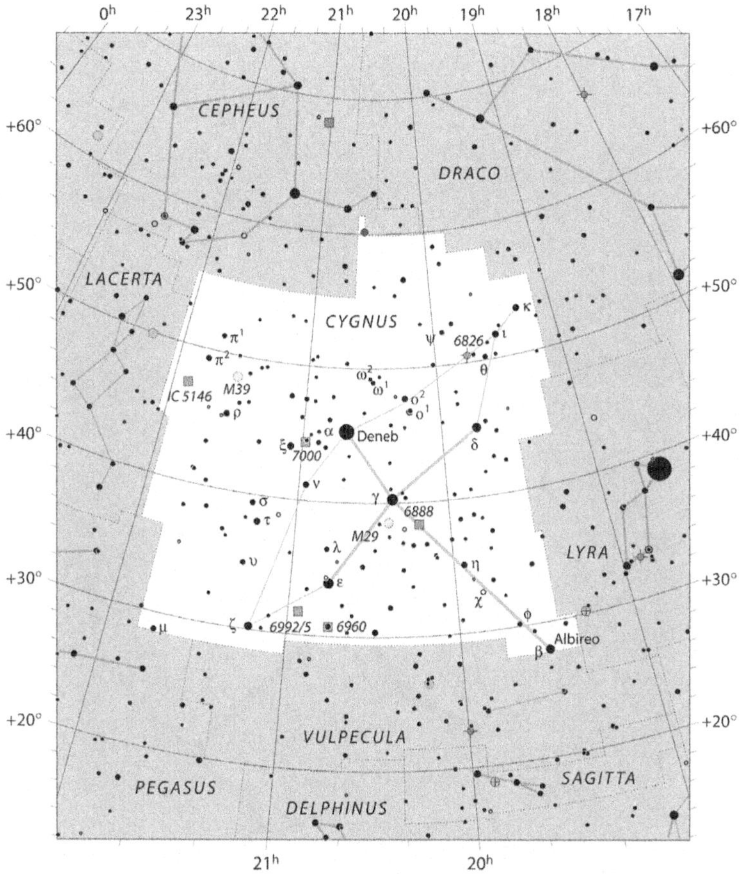

Figure 16. The constellation Cygnus.

The dancing woman was also associated with the appearance of the constellation Cygnus, which the Greeks called "Bird." Cygnus immediately preceded the dancer on October 19 and February 10, and followed the dancer three days later on April 28, and again four days later on June 17.

This brings to mind the iconography of Çatal Höyük. The cosmic dancer portrayed on a wall relief performed there at a time when the constellation Cygnus was rotating close to the North Pole. Both the Çatal Höyük dancer and the Phaistos dancer had long, whirling hair. The Phaistos dancer wore a long skirt covering her lower extremities. Neither spinning dancer had normal legs. The constellation Cygnus had no legs.

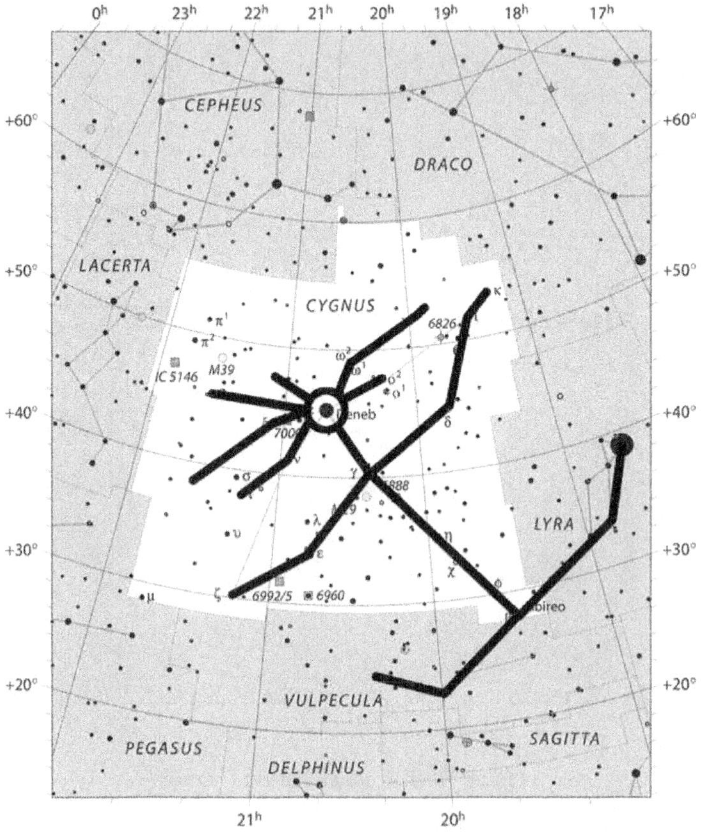

Figure 17. The constellation Cygnus, redrawn by the author.

Bare female legs. Venus rising in the east at dawn was present with another sign on the Disk, the pair of *bare woman's legs* disconnected from the body. This sign was associated with Venus.

Inverted triangle. The plain inverted triangle which appears at the center of Side B of the Disk is yet another sign of Venus: the pubis, also known as the Mound of Venus. It appeared near dawn in the east on sixteen occasions, and in the evening once, setting 8 a.m. on August 12.

Inverted triangle with dots. The inverted triangle, filled with dots, represents the female pubis full of seeds, and was also associated with the planet Venus, who was a fertility goddess. The triangle appears only on July 20, when Venus rose at 5 a.m. All five of the known planets were visible, Venus was in conjunction with the sun, and there was a new moon, another auspicious sign for fertility. This may have been thought the best day in the year for a couple to conceive a child.

Water signs. The man who appeared on March 9 coincided with the rise of Aquarius, the water carrier, at dawn in the east. The sign for a stream of water appeared seven times between March 5 and May 27, and all were correlated with significant positions of Aquarius.

Hanging fleece. The hanging fleece probably represented a sheep, rather than some other animal, since the wool of the sheep had long-lasting value. The palace at Pylos, a Minoan settlement in Greece, controlled 10,000 sheep (Barker 2005, 258). The fleece sign may have signaled times for slaughtering lambs, sheering wool, breeding sheep and processing wool. They are all correlated with positions of the constellation Aries.

Ram's head. The ram's head appeared just once, on April 30. This did not refer to breeding, since the breeding season of sheep is from October to early December. On April 30 the constellation Aries the Ram rose in the east at 4 a.m. It probably was connected with sheep-shearing or some other act of husbandry.

Dove. Doves mated and bred all year round. They were also seen as messengers between heaven and earth since they could fly very high. The dove was a symbol of the goddess Astarte (Ishtar) in Phoenicia. There was a shrine to a dove goddess at the Palace of Knossos of Crete. Later the Greeks sacrificed doves to Aphrodite (Venus). In a Cretan wedding song of today, the bride is represented by the dove. The dove sign was correlated with positions of the southern constellation Columba (dove) on October 23 and January 12.

Bull's horn. The bull's horn represented the bull, a symbol of power and masculinity. It played an important role in Minoan religion. The bull was the most expensive sacrifice made to the gods. The bull's horn appears on the Disk on July 1, October 15, November 4, November 23, December 20, and February 8. Perhaps on these days the Minoans engaged in bull-baiting sports, such as the gymnast vaulting the back of the bull. All these signs were correlated with positions of the visible constellation of the bull, Taurus.

Axe. The ominous axe, which appeared on July 15, suggested sacrifice. It seems likely that this was the date when the bull was killed. The appearance of the axe was correlated with the appearance at 7:00 a.m. of a lineup of all the known planets. Taurus, Gemini, and Orion peaked. The significance of these constellations was discussed in Chapter Three and will be discussed further in Chapter Six.

Eagle. On Side A the bull's horn was followed on all four appearances by an eagle, facing up, left, right, and then up. This sign represented the constellation of Aquila, the eagle of Zeus. This visible constellation moved in coordination with that of Taurus on the opposite horizon. Both were masculine symbols. In a Cretan wedding song the eagle represents the groom.

The eagle was also associated with the hammer, sign of the storm god. Zeus carried a staff; but Thor, his Scandinavian counterpart, carried a hammer. This sign, which occurred eight times on the Disk, was always correlated with positions of the planet Jupiter.

Hoof. The single hoof may represent the sure-footed goat. This sign appeared on November 16 and January 1. These two dates correspond to the setting of the constellation Capricorn, the sea goat, and its rise at dawn.

Fish. The fish sign was correlated with position of the constellation Pisces on the zodiac. These may have been auspicious days for fishing.

Dog. A dog's head appeared ten times on the Disk. Dogs were present in Minoan Crete, probably used for hunting and possibly for herding sheep. These signs without exception were correlated with positions of the constellations Canis Major and Canis Minor.

The dog's head on June 24 coincided with the rising of Sirius in Canis Major at 5 a.m. in the east. It was preceded by a jar and two beehive signs, June 21–23. This suggests a summer solstice festival in which honey was collected and offered to the gods (Kerenyi 1976, 118).

Ship. The best time for sailing today in the Aegean is from mid-April to the end of October. There is a week in January of good weather, when the winds die down. Sailing was represented by a ship sign on the Disk.

On Side B, a ship appeared on April 18, probably the beginning of the sailing season. On Side A there was a boat on November 20, the probable end of the season, and on January 5, during the probable week of good weather. There were no more ships until April 18, when the sailing season began again.

The appearance of ships in between April and November may have represented scheduled voyages with export goods for Egypt and elsewhere. They were correlated with positions of stars in Argo Navis, the large southern constellation in the southern sky of Crete, which included the subconstellations of Carina (keel), Puppis (poop), and Vela (sail). The ship signs on the Diskwere correlated with positions of Puppis and/or Vela.

The constellation Scorpius (Dionysos) appeared at the same times as the subconstellations Puppis and Vela of Argo Navis. According to myth, Dionysos traveled by ship spreading viniculture in the eastern Mediterranean.

Warrior. The head with the high brush of hair looks like that of a warrior. It was correlated with positions of the planet Mars (Ares). The Philistine soldiers in Palestine, who had a similar style are believed to have emigrated from Crete.

A layout of a building, perhaps the palace itself, is shown on Side A on September 6 and December 6. This sign may have designated feast days for all the personnel of the palace and their families. Both days were associated with unusual events in the sky. On September 6 the southern bright star Canopus just barely showed in the south, and the southern constellations were visible. On December 6 the constellations Scorpius (Dionysos) and Virgo, a wedded couple since October 17, peaked at 7 a.m.

Club. The club sign on the Disk suggested Herakles, who carried a club. Sure enough, all five occurrences of this sign were correlated with the location of the constellation of Hercules.

Runner. The runner, who appeared eight times on the Disk, was correlated with the positions of the constellation Boötes, which included Arcturus, the fourth brightest star in the sky. Arcturus was mentioned by Greek and Roman authors as a signal for undertaking agricultural work. Its name meant "guardian of the bears." Boötes was imagined as chasing two bears, Ursa Major and Ursa Minor. Without exception the runner sign was correlated with the positions of Boötes.

Lyre. The lyre, which appeared June 1 and July 7, was correlated with positions of the constellation Lyra.

Scales. The scales, which appeared October 24, were correlated with the rise of Libra in the east.

Bow. The bow, which appeared on January 8, was correlated with the rise of Sagittarius the archer in the east.

Pipes. Pan was a Greek god of fertility, the son of Hermes. He played his pipes to mourn the loss of a nymph he loved. The panpipes, January 24 and 28, were correlated with the setting of Virgo in the west at dawn.

Ragged piece. A difficult sign to decipher was a ragged or torn piece of something (July 8) when Virgo set at 7 p.m. The torn piece of something may have represented the torn hymen of Virgo. At that hour Jupiter was passing out of Virgo and making conjunction with Saturn.

Cymbal. The cymbal, which people strike to get attention, appeared on October 18, when Saturn and Mars were in conjunction at dawn.

Man amazed. The man who stood amazed (?) on August 7 at 6 a.m. may represent Boötes viewing the lineup of the five planets and Gemini and Orion at peak.

Grouping in segments. After interpreting all the individual signs on the Disk, the possible reasons for grouping them into segments of two to fifteen days each were considered. Some segments could be explained in astrological terms. Astrologers hold that Mercury is the ruling planet of the constellation Virgo; that Venus is the ruler of Taurus, the Mars is the ruler of Aries, and that Jupiter is the ruler of Pisces. Those pairs of signs occurred together repeatedly in the same division of the Disk.

Spiral. Finally one must ask why the maker of the Disk decided to design it as a spiral. Kerenyi argues that the original design of the labyrinth in the palace of Knossos was not a square but a spiral. This was probably the most sacred place in the Cretan religion. On a coin of Knossos of the fifth century B.C.E. a four-part labyrinth is depicted connected with a star in the center. This may have been a hint that the movements of the stars and planets governed the Minoan religion (Kerenyi 1976, 91–92).

Why was the spiral pattern chosen? One candidate was a mollusk called the conch, known to the Minoans both in natural form and reproductions. The origin of the name is Greek: *conche*, probably pronounced konkha. There are many big spiral shells in existence; the most likely candidate is *Strombus decorus raybaudii*. If the apex is removed from a conch shell and one blows through it, the shell will produce loud, weird sounds. Perhaps it was used as a foghorn or in the more solemn rituals of the Cretan religion (Montagu 1981). It is also possible that the Minoans ate the soft tissues of this mollusk out of season, when it contained neurotoxins, and experienced hallucinations and euphoria as a result (Glowacki 2005). The spiral may also represent a spiritual passage, or growth and development. (In India the Mother Goddess is depicted holding a conch shell, usually interpreted as a symbol of change or becoming.)

Conclusion

The evidence presented here supports the view that the Phaistos Disk was a solar calendar. It also seems likely that the Minoans invented many of the northern constellations in use today.

The methodology used for this decipherment was to reconstruct the night sky over Phaistos in the year 1613 B.C.E., using the computer program *Your Sky*. The signs on the Disk were treated as pictograms. These pictograms were found to have correlates among the stars and planets, in agricultural operations, and possibly in religious rituals.

The decipherment of the Phaistos Disk supports the view that the Minoans created eleven of the zodiac constellations in the seventeenth century B.C.E.

References

Aveni, Anthony. 2000. *Empires of Time*. Boulder: University Press of Colorado.

Barker, Graeme, 2005, Agriculture, pastoralism, and Mediterranean landscapes in prehistory." *The Archaeology of Mediterranean*

Prehistory. Ed. Emma Burke and E. Bernard Knapp. Oxford: Blackwell. 270–274.

Black, Jeremy and Anthony Green. 1992. *Gods, Demons and Symbols of Ancient Mesopotamia.* Austin: University of Texas.

Brown, David. 2000. *Mesopotamian Planetary Astronomy-Astrology.* Gronigen: Styx.

Fitton, J. Lesley. 2002. *The Minoans.* London: Cambridge University Press.

Friedlander, Walter J. 1992. *The Golden Wand of Medicine: A History of the Caduceus Symbol in Medicine.* Westport, CT: Greenwood Press.

Friedrich, Walter L. et al. 2006. "Santorini eruption radiocarbon dated to 1627–1600 B.C.E., " *Science* V: 312 (28 April). 548.

Glowacki, Mary. 2005. "Food of the Gods or mere mortals?" *Antiquity* 79 (304). 257–268.

Goodison, Lucy and Christine Morris. 1998. "Beyond the Great Mother: the sacred world of the Minoans." *Ancient Goddesses,* ed. Goodison and Morris. London: British Museum Press.

Hannah, Robert. 2005. *Greek and Roman Calendars.* London: Duckworth.

Henriksson, Göran, and Mary Blomberg. 1996. "Evidence for Minoan astronomical observations from the peak structures on Petsophas and Graostalos," *Opuscula Atheniensia* XXI: 6. 99–114.

———. 2011. "The evidence from Knossos on the Minoan calendar." *Mediterranean Archeology and Archaeometry* 11:1. 59–68.

Kerenyi, Carl. 1976. *Dionysos.* Princeton: Princeton University Press.

Manning, Stuart W. et. al. 2006. "Chronology for the Aegean Late Bronze Age, 1700–1400 BC." *Science,* V: 312 (28 April). 565–569.

McGovern, Patrick. 2003. *Ancient Wine.* Princeton: Princeton University Press.

Merlin, Mark D. 1984. *On the Trail of the Ancient Opium Poppy.* Rutherford, N. J.: Farleigh Dickinson Press.

Montagu, Jeremy. 1981. "The conch in prehistory." *World Archaeology* 12 (3). 273–279.

Ovenden, Michael. 1966. "The origin of the constellations," *The Philosophical Journal* 3. 1–18.

Pomerance, Leon. 1976. *The Phaistos Disc.* Goteborg: Paul Astroms.

Pratt, John. 2001. "Scientifically Dating the Constellations," "Zodiac" history, Wikipedia, fn 5.

Schaefer, Bradley F. 2006. "The origin of the Greek constellations," *Scientific American* (November) 96–101.

Taylour, William and John Chadwick. 2004. *The Mycenaeans.* London: Cambridge University Press.

Willetts, R. F. 1977. *The Civilization of Ancient Crete.* New York: Phoenix Press.

Chapter Six

Minoan Religion

Some Solutions to Problems in Greek Mythology

The proposed decipherment of the Phaistos Disk provides possible solutions to some problems connected with Greek mythology and religion.

1. Seasonal changes, heralded by movements of stars, determined the timing of the festivals of Dionysos in Crete and later in Greece. The prominence of Dionysos in Greek religion, involving the use of wine, can be traced back to Minoan religion and wine production.

2. The role of the astral boat (Argo Navis) in the southern sky serves to explain why Dionysos "arrived" in various parts of Greece on a "boat." The constellation "Scorpius" (Dionysos?) and the three parts of the astral boat (Puppis, Vela, and Carina) rose and set near the southern horizon.

3. The Cretans may have made ritual use of opium. Hermes was a patron of opium production and use. Perhaps the swift messenger took opium users on "trips." The love goddess accompanied them.

4. The Cretan origin of Zeus may be supported by the appearance of the hammer sign on the Disk and its correlation with positions of Jupiter in the sky. The Greeks associated Zeus with the planet Jupiter. However in Crete Zeus was not a pre-eminent sky patriarch or the head of a pantheon. He used his hammer to make thunder.

5. Hercules with his club, Boötes the bear guardian, and perhaps Pan with his pipes may have been present in Minoan mythology.

Four of the known planets, each linked to a deity, were represented on the Disk: Hermes (Mercury), Ares (Mars), Aphrodite (Venus), and Zeus (Jupiter).

6. The symbolic animals of Minoan Crete were the bull, eagle, ram, dove, dog, bee, goat, and fish, all of which had celestial correlates.

7. The dancing woman on the Disk may be a descendant of the cosmic dancer found at Çatal Höyük, Anatolia, in the seventh millennium B.C.E. In both cases they were associated with the movement of the constellation Cygnus, symbolized on the Disk by a horizontal V, perhaps a symbol of migrating birds. Two appearances of the dancer on the Disk were preceded by the latter symbol (10–20, 2–11). The third appearance of the dancer was followed by this symbol three days later (4–25), and its fourth appearance was followed by the symbol four days later (6–13).

8. Based on the proposed decipherment of the Disk it is possible to identify three days out of 360 that may have been occasions for major religious rituals.

9. The appearance of the axe on July 15 when Orion the Hunter was at his peak with Taurus in the east, was ominous and may have been the occasion for bull sacrifice.

10. The palace signs suggested a major gathering of Minoans in the Phaistos area. On September 6, the appearance of the palace coincided with the appearance of the bright star Canopus on the southern horizon. The second appearance of the "palace" on December 6 coincided with the appearance of Scorpius, Virgo, and Corona Borealis at their peak. This may have been a celebration of the mating of Dionysos and Ariadne (Persephone?) occurring on October 17.

This decipherment of the Phaistos Disk presents evidence that the Minoans deserve credit for inventing many of the principal northern hemisphere constellations now in use, and that the Babylonians may have learned much from the Minoans.

The Image of the Lady

Where was Potnia, "The Lady" or "Our Lady " the powerful Nature goddess acknowledged by scholars to be dominant in Minoan Crete? What form did She have? Did She have a celestial correlate?

In Minoan art Her legs and sometimes Her feet were well covered with a long full skirt. Her breasts were often bared. (The same was true of Her Minoan female worshippers.) She sometimes had no facial features. She was reminiscent of the pregnant Paleolithic and Neolithic female icons except that She had a wasp-waist, like that of a honeybee, and also like that of Orion.

As argued above, the pregnant, faceless and footless female images of prehistoric times had a celestial correlate: Her form in the sky was "The Central Woman" (*al-Jauza'*) who may have been equivalent approximately to the constellation "Gemini." (See Chapter Two.) The two outstanding stars in that constellation, the pair Castor and Pollux, may have been interpreted as Her breasts or possibly, her eyes. They were seen as a pair because they were about the same magnitude and fairly close to each other. They were also very bright and located in the brightest part of the night sky. No other pair of stars in the northern sky met these criteria. Immediately below them runs the Milky Way into which Her milk appeared to flow.

There are no Twins on the Phaistos Disk. When the constellation of "Gemini" appeared in a significant position in the sky, on the Disk a hand wrapped in cloth appeared in an upheld position, suggesting the making of an oath, as some Middle East merchants do. The Minoan name of Potnia (The Lady) was a secret. Perhaps when the Minoans made oaths in her name they did so silently.

The Potnia had no equally powerful or more powerful male consort. The Greek goddesses Gaia, Rhea, and Hera were consorts of a superior patriarchal deity. So were Hathor, Isis, and Asherah. Demeter's position was ambiguous. But ancient Neith, the sky goddess of Egypt had no male consort, and Inanna (Ishtar, Astarte) had only disposable lovers. No god has been mentioned as the consort of the pagan Arab goddess al-Ilat, whose name meant "The Goddess." So the Cretan goddess was not the only one without a consort.

It may be that scholars who imagined The Lady of Minoan Crete to be an Earth Goddess, or "Mother Earth," were on the wrong track. Neither was she a Sky Goddess in the sense of the whole sky, like Nut of Egypt. She may have been found in a specific group of stars that included Gemini. She didn't need legs: she was flying up in the sky. Minoan priestesses may have worn long skirts and bared their breasts in imitation of Her.

Orion and Minoan Symbolism

Next let us examine the constellation Orion, which was also called al-Jauza' by some Arabs. According to the Persian astronomer Abd-al-Rahman al-Sufi (903–986 C.E.), Al-Jauza' in early Arabia was a female. She was at one time married to the princely star Canopus (Suhail) when Canopus was located north of its present location, nearer to today's Orion. According to a myth, Canopus fled to the south to get away from his wife (Allen 1899, 69). This serves to support the idea that the female Orion was a death goddess.

Sometimes the Arabs gave the name al-Jauza' to just the bright stars in Orion's belt, or to the star Betelgeuse only.

The Greeks said that Orion was the grandson of Minos, king of Crete. While hunting in Crete he became a threat to the life of every beast on earth. So the hunter was hunted by a scorpion sent by the Gaia the Earth Goddess. The scorpion bit him on the heel, and he died. The constellation Scorpius rose in the east shortly after Orion set in the west, which was the symbolic equivalent of dying. So Orion

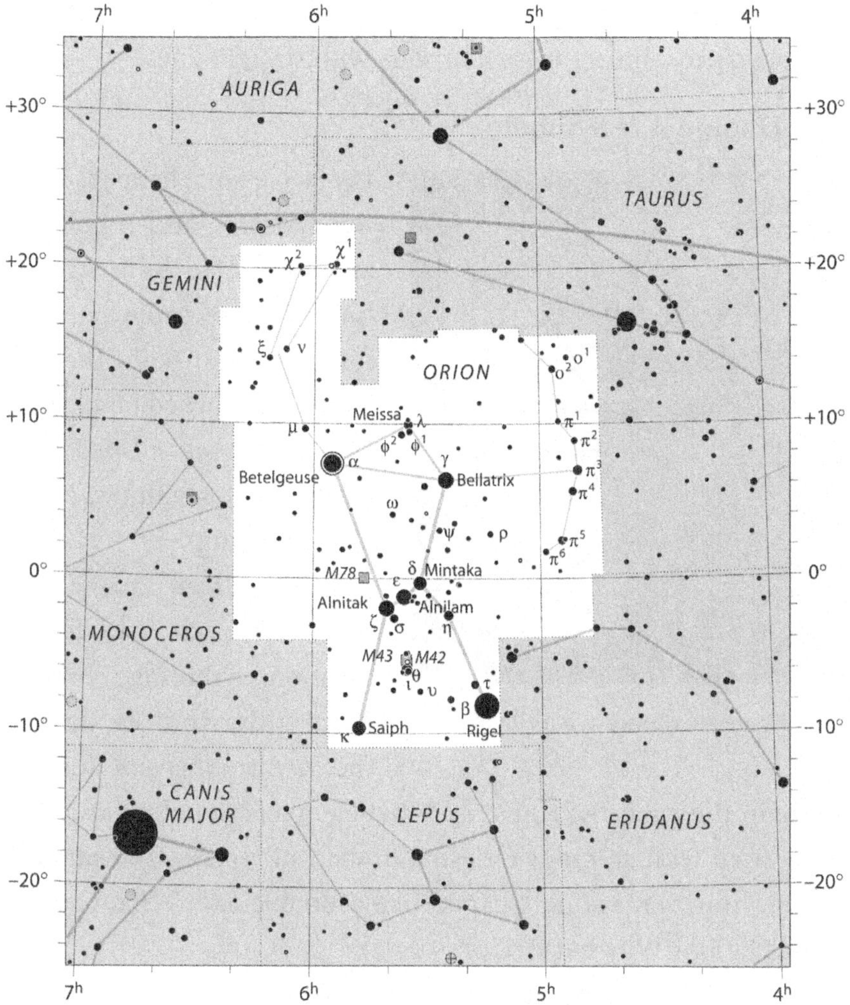

Figure 18. The constellation Orion.

both inflicted and suffered violent death. His enemy was Dionysos (Scorpius ?), the reborn god, the god of wine and joy.

The stars representing Orion's arms and weapons are faint. His right arm is raised, the left is extended to the side. Orion has no face. In myth he was temporarily blinded. His torso and thighs are outlined by four bright stars: Betelgeuse (*Beit al-Jauza, the House of the Central Woman*, in Arabic), Bellatrix (female warrior, in Latin),

Rigel (leg, in Arabic), and Saiph (or Saif, sword, in Arabic). It is customary to connect these four stars with straight lines.

The Double Axe Symbol

Figure 19. Hunter, Çatal Höyük.

Let us see what happens when Betelgeuse and Bellatrix are connected by a straight line. Let the same be done for Rigel and Saif. Then let "Orion" be turned on his side. *"Orion" becomes a Double Axe* (two triangles with two points only touching).

The Greek name for the double axe was *labrys*, meaning "shining, bright." From this word is derived the name *labyrinth* for the maze in the palace of Knossos. What elements in nature are most associated with shining? Celestial bodies, of course. The sun and moon, however, are not shaped like a double axe. What about a constellation? Why not Orion?

The double axe in Minoan Crete was shown only in the hands of a woman. The real axe for killing the bull was probably like the single bladed axe shown on the Phaistos Disk.

But the double axe is shown over a bull's head in a late Minoan vase from eastern Crete.

Orion's astral bow is pointed toward Taurus the Bull. Orion was seen as a threat to the Bull.

The earliest double axe was found in the sixth millennium B.C.E. in the northern Mesopotamian town of Arapchiyah (Settegast 2005, 51). Ritual double axes made of stone and amber have been found in Northern European Megalithic tombs of the fourth and third millennia B.C.E. (Gimbutas 1991, 268). A double axe was portrayed in the Hittite site at Boğazköy (formerly Hattusas, the Hittite capital, now known as Boğazkale) in central Anatolia (later second millennium). The double axe was held by a youth standing on a feline immediately behind the Hittite Great Goddess (Frazer, 1914, 137–138). As for the feline, it may be the "leopard," Canis Major, which includes the brightest star in the sky, Sirius (see Chapter Two).

In modern times the Greeks had a word *astropeleki* or "star axe" for a stone shaped like an axe head that they might find outdoors. They believed it was a weapon of the thunder god thrown to earth. It was valued as magical and handed down from father to son (Blinkenberg 1987, 107).

It appears that the suggestion that the double axe was a butterfly or a symbol of rebirth was not quite right. The double axe may have symbolized death, while the butterfly, shaped like two triangles conjoined, may have symbolized the soul escaping the body after death (Gimbutas 1989, 273–75).

Orion and Hekate

Orion has some remarkable similarities with the Greek goddess, Hekate, whose name means "The Hundred One" (*hekaton* = 100). Hekate, like Potnia, is not a proper name but an attribute of the goddess. She is considered pre-Greek; when Zeus came to power he "allowed" her to keep her traditional powers (Johnstone 2005, 3899–3900).

1. Like Orion, Hekate was associated with Death. She guarded the door to the Underworld. She was the Queen of Ghosts. She was sometimes portrayed with a rope and a knife, symbolizing the separation of body and soul at death and/or the separation of earth and sky.

Curiously, the bright star Bellatrix in Orion, meaning "female warrior," is also connected with death. But why a female warrior in a male constellation? Perhaps "Bellatrix" is a remnant of the Death Goddess.

2. Like Orion, Hekate was associated with dogs. Orion had two: Canis Major and Canis Minor. These constellations were close to both Orion and Gemini. Hekate's dogs barked at night when she moved about.

3. Orion is made up of stars. Hekate was the daughter of Asteria, an obscure Greek star goddess whose name means "starry."

4. Orion's right arm is shown raised, supposedly holding a club. His left arm is extended and attached to a vertical semi-circle of stars, believed to be a bow. Images of a female with one arm up and one arm down have been found in Neolithic Hungary, Bulgaria, Poland and Sardinia (Gimbutas, 1989, 16–17; 1991, 240).

One of Hekate's arms was sometimes depicted as raised, holding a torch. One of her epithets was *phosphoros:* light-bringer.

However, another interpretation is possible: the upraised right arm is typical of a spinner (a female occupation). Her right hand holds the fibers, pulling them in parallel lines out of a distaff of tow, and twisting them. Her left arm is extended from her side, holding the thread attached to the spindle, and flicking the wrist to keep the spindle rotating.

In the prehistoric and ancient world, spinning had magical significance. In the analogical thinking of the time, there was a connection between spinning and the creation of body tissue. Spinning involved the twisting of fibers to make a thread and the winding of them around a spindle. It may be the origin of the metaphor, "the thread of life."

The word "tissue" originally meant "something woven." The fetus is attached to the mother by the umbilical cord. By means of the cord it may be imagined that the thread of life is wound around its spine, adding on body tissue. This was the kind of magic that only a woman could perform. The Greek verb, "to spin," is *neo,* the Latin verb is *nere,* The Greek word for new or young was *neos*, the word for womb was *nedos* (Suhr 1967, 30–36 and 75; Onians 1951 395–419).

Frigg, the Nordic wife of Odin, was a sky goddess. She possessed a distaff, now seen as part of Orion's belt. Alternatively, her distaff may be the Y-shaped constellation of Cancer. Frigg also had a drop spindle, possibly the two-star constellation of Canis Minor nearby. Her work was to spin and weave clouds.

Another clue to Orion's original identity is his association in Greek mythology with bees. His birthplace, Hyrai, was derived from the Cretan word for a swarm of bees, or a beehive. The decipherment of the Phaistos Disk shows the constellation Orion as a correlate of the honeybee sign. Like the honeybee, Orion is wasp-waisted. But the honeybee, whose leader is a queen, was associated with the goddesses: Neith (Egyptian), Hannahanna (Hittite) and Demeter (Greek). What does a hunter of animals have to do with bees?

A possible solution is that Orion and his myth were a later invention masking the original female identity of the constellation "Orion."

The Triple Goddess

Hekate was sometimes portrayed as a triple goddess. More precisely, she was seen as a member of a holy trinity consisting of the Virgin (Virgo), the Mother (Potnia) and the Crone (Hekate). She was mentioned in the Demeter-Persephone myth as the one who returned Persephone to her Mother (Ann and Imel 1993, 179).

As for the significance of the name Hekate, derived from Greek *hekaton* (one hundred), this may be sought by reconstructing the sky over Athens (38 degrees latitude, 24 degrees longitude) in 600 B.C.E. and by following the course of the constellation Orion. On May 15

Orion was completely visible at dawn. On August 13, a feast-day for Hekate, Orion was at his peak at dawn. On August 24, Orion was just beyond his peak at dawn. *The period May 15 to August 24 consisted of one hundred days.*

What then does the "one hundred" attribute of Hekate signify? It was a time of the death of vegetation during the rainless period. It may also have been a time of contagious disease epidemics. Both Hekate and Orion were associated with Death. Death was believed to have the greatest influence in the period between Orion's rising in the east, and his peak, or culmination. Hekate appears to have represented Orion at his most dangerous.

One can check this Athens calendar calculation against the decipherment of the Phaistos Disk. On July 15, 1613 B.C.E. in Phaistos Orion was at his peak. The sign for that day was an axe (single, not double). This suggested sacrifice and danger. Probably the bull was killed then.

Now one can consider the meaning of the "horns of consecration." Oliver Pelon and Nanno Marinatos have suggested that they represent twin peaks with a space in between (Pelon and Marinatos 2005, 40). This is probably correct. Sometimes the double axe is shown above the space between the peaks. It may be rising over a notch in the horizon used as a marker for the rising or setting of stars. In Phaistos the "horns of consecration" may have indicated the twin peaks of Mt. Ida to the north. The practice of placing the double axe over the gap between the peaks would have been to indicate the rising or setting of Orion or his ominous female counterpart.

The Life and Death of the Minoan Religion

It is now possible to make a tentative construction of the locations of the three aspects of the tripartite Great Goddess imagined by Robert Graves (Graves, 1960, 92 fn.). She was Virgin, Mother, and Crone. In the sky she was Virgo (the Virgin), "Gemini" (the mother, the

Central Woman), and "Orion" (the crone, Hekate, also called the Central Woman). The goddess Hekate and the Orion of myth may have been inspired by the same constellation. The double axe symbol may have been inspired by the central figure of Orion seen sideways.

The Failure of the Minoan Civilization

Minoan Crete in the Bronze Age enjoyed a relatively stable maritime climate. It was protected by its navy and the sea all around it. The Time of Trouble (2200–400 B.C.E.) disturbed this arrangement because drought, migrations, and invasions brought insecurity to all the countries of the eastern Mediterranean.

In part, Minoan religion disappeared with the rest of Minoan civilization when volcanic eruptions and earthquakes, particularly at the island of Thera (Santorini) from c. 1628 to c.1450 B.C.E. destroyed ships, buildings, and people on Crete on a massive scale. The Greek invaders then inserted their own culture there. But it is curious that so much was buried and forgotten. Greek mythology is full of mysteries and ambiguities in connection with Cretan material.

It seems reasonable to suppose that the male-dominant religions that took over Crete suppressed the Minoan female-dominated religion. In part, this must have been facilitated by Greek introduction of trained horses into Crete at the end of the second millennium.

But the Phaistos Disk also suggests that Minoan religion had an inherent weakness: the use of opium. Opium is very habit-forming. It destroys its addicts. The Minoans probably produced enough for export. If there is no resistance to opium use, it can undermine political and military power. The opium factor may help to explain the disappearance of Minoan religion from the scene.

Unlike opium the ergot-based hallucinogens known to Indo-Europeans were not addictive because they were available for only a short time during the year and could not be preserved in the primitive forms of storage available.

References

Allen, Richard Hinckley. 1899. *Star Names and their Meanings.* New York: E. E. Stechert.

Allouche, Adel. 2005. "Arabian Religion," *Encyclopedia of Religion,* vol. 1, 442–446.

Ann, Martha, and Dorothy Myers Imel. 1993. *Goddesses in World Mythology.* Santa Barbara: ABC Clio.

Bayley, Clinton. 1974. "Bedouin Star-Lore in Sinai and the Negev," *Bulletin of the School of Oriental and African Studies,* 37, 580–596.

Blinkenberg, Christian. 1987. *The Thunder Weapon in Religion and Folklore.* New Rochele, N.Y.: Caratzas.

Frazer, James G. 1914. *Adonis, Attis, Osiris.* Third ed. New Hyde Park, N.Y.: University Books.

Gimbutas, Marija. 1989. *The Language of the Goddess.* San Francisco; Harper.

———. 1991. *The Civilization of the Goddess.* San Francisco: Harper.

Graves, Robert. 1960. *The Greek Myths.* London, Penguin.

Johnstone, Sarah. 2005. "Hekate," *Encyclopedia of Religion,* vol. 6, 3899–3900.

Marinatos, Nanno. 1993. *Minoan Religion; Ritual, Image, and Symbol.* Columbia, S.C.: University of South Carolina Press.

Nilsson, Martin P. 1950. *The Minoan-Mycenaean Religion and its Survival in Greek Religion.* Second ed. Lund: W. K. Gleerup.

Onians, Richard B. 1951. *The Origins of European Thought.* London; Cambridge University Press.

Pelon, Oliver, and Nanno Marinatos. 2003. "Aegean Religions," *Encyclopedia of Religion,* vol. 1, 37–44.

Settegast, Mary. 2003. *When Zarathustra Spoke.* 2005. Costa Mesa, Calif.: Mazda.

Suhr, Elmer G. 1967. *The Spinning Aphrodite.* New York; Helios.

Varisco, Daniel M. 2000. "Islamic Folk Astronomy." *Astronomy Across Cultures,* ed, Helaine Selin. Dordrecht: Kluwer. 615–650.

Chapter Seven

Mystery Cults of the Ancient World

Greek Religion in General

Mature Greek religion was almost completely humanized: the god Pan was the only animal deity. The other deities all had very human faults. The male gods were adulterers and rapists. Venus was promiscuous; Mars was violent. Many were jealous and vengeful. But that was beside the point: each had a certain kind of power which the Greeks believed might be helpful to humans.

The deities also had mythical animal companions. The bull was associated with Zeus, Poseidon, and Dionysos. The ram or goat was linked to Hermes; the stag, to Apollo and Artemis; the dog, to Hekate and Orion; the eagle, to Zeus; the owl, to Athena; the dove, to Aphrodite; and the honeybee, to Demeter and Orion. Hercules wore the skin and skull of a lion. Dionysos wore a leopard skin. Helios and Poseidon acquired horse associations (Burkert 1985, 64–65).

Although their deities did not serve as moral role models. the Greeks had moral standards. They condemned incest, perjury, and violations of the rules of hospitality. Wrongdoing, they felt, would "pollute" them or their families. The Greeks valued justice (Ferguson 2003, 156). They respected the military virtues, bravery and loyalty, which were clearly expressed in Homer's epic poems.

The religion of the Greeks reflected their family organization. Their gods were a family in which all the members had some power. Zeus, the patriarch, was neither omnipotent nor entirely benevolent.

Thus the Greeks were able to explain—without blaming a satanic deity—why bad things happened to good people: the gods had vices and even some good humans acted with arrogance (*hubris*).

The Greeks loved wine, which they poured out as a libation to their gods. The cult of Dionysos, god of wine, was strong in Athens, but the Greeks might serve wine at any holy festival: theirs was a "wet" religion.

Did the Greeks use any other drugs for religious purposes?

By the fourth century B.C.E., Greek "mystery" cults offered ecstasy on earth, community in worship, and happiness in the afterlife. The two most interesting cults were those of Demeter and Dionysos.

The Cult of Demeter

The most famous Goddess cult among the ancient Greeks was that of Demeter at Eleusis, fifteen miles away from Athens. Beginning in 1500 B.C.E., the cult lasted almost two thousand years—almost as long as Christianity and longer than Islam.

The priestesses of Demeter probably purveyed at least two psychoactive substances. Opium was celebrated in temple iconography, and *kykeon,* a stimulating mixed drink, was served to thousands in the annual fall ritual at the temple.

Excavations at Eleusis have revealed that the temple of Demeter was built around 1500 B.C.E. (Cosmopoulos 2003, 1). The principal source of information about the cult is the seventh-century B.C.E. *Hymn to Demeter* (Foley 1994, 68).

According to the *Hymn,* the sacred drink was composed of barley, water, and "herbs" (often translated as "mint"). The hymnodist says, "I know the powerful great herbs we gathered and the talisman plant that wards off possession." A talisman is something with magic or miraculous effects. "Possession" probably refers to "demonic possession," a label given to mental illness. So at least one of the ingredients in *kykeon* was probably psychoactive.

Demeter was the goddess of cereal agriculture. She also personified maternal love. Consequently she played the role in Greek religion that the Virgin Mary plays in Christianity.

The cult of Demeter was related to the seasonal cycle. The Greeks, who lived in an arid Mediterranean climate like that of California, divided the year into a hot dry season of four months, from mid-May to mid-September, and an eight-month wet season. In the dry season, vegetation died back, except for deep-rooted plants such as the fig, olive, and grape. Cereal crops were sown in the wet season.

Also told in the *Hymn* is the myth of Persephone (Kore), daughter of Demeter. In the spring, Persephone (Kore) and other girls were out picking flowers. All was well until Persephone picked a narcissus, whereupon Hades, god of the Underworld, emerged from a crack in the earth, seized her, and took her down to his kingdom. There he persuaded her to eat pomegranate seeds, the food of the dead. (The number of seeds varies with the telling: one, four, or six.)

Demeter grieved so much for the loss of her daughter that she stopped eating nectar and ambrosia, the food of the gods. Refusing wine, she asked for *kykeon*. The earth became infertile; no food plants grew; and the people stopped sacrificing to the gods.

Wandering the barren earth near Corinth, Demeter came to Mekone, or "Poppy Town," where the gods caused poppies to spring up beneath her feet. As she knelt to look at the flowers, their overpowering fragrance caused her to fall asleep, releasing her from grief. Today, farmers harvesting poppy seed capsules often feel dizzy from the scent.

Importuned by the other gods, Zeus decreed that Persephone was to spend only a portion of each year in Hades, corresponding to the number of pomegranate seeds she had eaten there. In one version of the myth, Persephone lived with Hades four months: that is, the dry season from mid-May to mid-August. In another version of the myth, she was in the Underworld for six months: in other words, mid-February to mid-August, when the constellation Virgo was below the horizon. Hades and Demeter accepted this compromise and Persephone returned to her mother. The crops grew again.

The principal ritual of the cult of Demeter was in the fall, probably in early September, during the month of Boedromion. Barley and wheat were planted at this time, and (in the era of Hesiod, about 800 B.C.E.) the rains were expected.

The fall ritual of the cult of Demeter, called the Greater Mysteries, was an initiation ritual. All adults except murderers were allowed to participate. The original purpose of the ritual was probably to guarantee the continued growth of the crops. But by the fourth century B.C.E. the ritual was believed to provide its participants a happy afterlife. The Greeks felt the ritual was of highest importance and they celebrated it regularly, year after year.

The Athenians who wanted to participate in the festivities had to travel the fifteen miles to Eleusis. After some preliminaries they had to spend two days fasting. They broke their fast by drinking *kykeon* on the 20–21 of Boedromium, gathered in the great hall of the temple for rituals. The exact nature of these rituals was secret. Probably the best source on the character of the rituals was a lost work of Plutarch, *On the Soul,* of which only a fragment survives.

At first the initiates, who may have been blindfolded, experienced terror, with shivering, trembling, sweating, and utter amazement. Then they saw a strange and brilliant light, after which they entered a delightful environment: with clean and verdant meadows, gentle voices, choric dances, and other visions. The initiates joined in the revelry, feeling that their soul was free of the body. When the effects of the *kykeon* wore off, the initiates took another kind of drink, also mysterious, and felt blissful (Stobaeus 4.52.49).

In 300 B.C.E. Athens took over the Eleusinian Mysteries, and the number of initiates greatly increased. The cult lasted until 392 C.E., when the Byzantine emperor, Theodosius I, closed the sanctuaries of Demeter. The invading Goths destroyed and desecrated the sites in 396 C.E.

The reference to a sudden, prolonged period in which food crops could not grow may have been related to a historic event. At some point in the period 1627–1600 B.C.E. there was a disastrous eruption of the volcano on the island of Thera (Santorini) in the Aegean Sea. This eruption is now ranked as a category seven out of a possible seven in the severity of its explosion (see Chapter Five). Other eruptions followed in 1500 and 1450.

An eruption of this size was likely to send clouds of sulfuric oxide gas to the stratosphere, where it would block the sun's rays from reaching the earth. Such an eruption could have caused a "year without a summer" with famine, followed by additional chilly years of subnormal crop yields. That was what happened when the volcano Tambora erupted in 1815 at the category seven level of explosivity.

The same kind of event may have affected Anatolia, for according to a Hittite myth, the Sun God suddenly disappeared, causing a paralyzing frost (Hoffman 1990, 26).

Sudden climatic adversity may have been the original and ongoing motivation for the Demeter cult rituals at Eleusis and elsewhere in the area starting around 1500 B.C.E.

One of the epithets of Demeter was "healer." The priestesses of the cult may have been exceptionally well-informed about the medicinal and psychoactive properties of the herbs available in Greece. Statues of Demeter show her holding poppy blooms along with ears of barley or wheat. On a metal vessel for serving drinks are found drawings of many poppy capsules. There are many four and eight petalled rosettes on the artifacts of Eleusis representing the crown of the poppy capsule (Kerenyi 1967, 74 ff.).

Opium (*Papaver somniferum*) has been considered as a possible ingredient in *kykeon*. But opium depresses the central nervous system. Opium produced a feeling of bliss and then sleepiness. It might have been given at the end of the main drug experience. But the mystery drug in *kykeon* caused a feeling of awakening. It must have been a stimulant and probably a hallucinogen.

Demeter was associated with the queen bee. Her priestesses were called *melissae*, or bees. They probably engaged in apiculture and fermented honey by adding two parts water to one part honey, containing the natural yeast *Saccharomyces cerevisiae*, to make mead, an alcoholic drink. This was the same yeast found naturally as a bloom on grapes. Both honey and mead could have been useful to offset the bitter taste of opium.

There have been many suggestions in the last fifty years as to the identity of the secret ingredient in *kykeon*. One suggestion was that the barley used in the drink had been colonized by *Claviceps purpurea,* the microfungal source of hallucinogenic ergot alkaloids. But this fungus rarely colonizes any cereal in the field except rye. Wheat and barley, not rye, were the staple cereals of Greece.

Another candidate ingredient in *kykeon* is the drug Homer called *moly.* Homer mentioned it in Book 10 of the *Odyssey*. This work was probably written in the eighth century B.C.E., although the events it depicts may have taken place centuries earlier.

Odysseus and his men arrived at the forested isle of Aiolia. The island belonged to Circe (Kirke), a beautiful goddess with a knowledge of drugs. Odysseus sent a scouting party of 23 men out and they come to the "sacred palace" of Circe. She invited them in for food and drink, and 22 accepted; the remaining man was suspicious and waited outside.

Circe gave her guests a drink of wine in which she puts barley, cheese, green honey, and a "baneful drug" so that they "entirely forgot their dear homeland." They turned into pigs; she put them in a pen and fed them pig food (the fruit of ilex and cornel). The man who was suspicious and had waited outside saw what had happened and returned to Odysseus with the sad tale. Hermes came to the aid of Odysseus with a "noble" and "excellent" plant called *moly.* Its root was black and its flowers were white. It was very hard to dig up.

Apparently after taking this drug Odysseus went to the palace of Circe and she invited him in. She gave him a drink with a drug in it, but he was not affected. She took a wand and ordered him to go to the pigpen with the rest of his comrades. He pulled his sword and rushed toward her as if to kill her.

She fell on her knees in front of him and invited him to come to her bed and lie with her. He asked her to swear an oath that she would not try to do him any evil. She agreed; the bedding followed; but he refused to eat and drink with her until she freed his men. She let the men out of the pigpen and gave them another drug to counteract the baneful one. They turned back into men, but were younger, larger, and more handsome than before.

The "baneful" drug that Circe gave the 22 men was probably opium dissolved in wine. It was sleep inducing and since it was an aphrodisiac could have turned men into "animals." The Greeks believed that after a deep sleep with dreams—such as an opium-induced sleep—a man could wake up feeling youthful and looking more handsome.

In Book 4 of Homer's Odyssey there is a mention of *nepenthes,* which is also thought to have been opium. It was probably the drug which Helen *added to wine* and gave to Telemachus and his comrades to ease their grief over losses in the Trojan War (Homer 2002 IV, 117; X, 210–215).

The second drug used by Circe was probably a stimulant. The *moly* plant appears to have been *Peganum harmala*, or wild rue. Wild rue has five-petalled white flowers, and a black tap root that may go down four feet or more, making it difficult to pull up.

Figure 20. Five-petalled flower of wild rue *(Peganum harmala).*

The plant called *moly* turned up also in the herbal of Dioscorides in the first century B.C.E. *Moly* is an alternate name, used in Anatolia, for his *Peganon agrion.* The name *moly* continued to turn up in medieval and renaissance herbals of Europe (Stannard 1999, 254–307). The seeds of wild rue are in a fruit that is ripe in late summer or early fall, just in time for the Greater Mysteries. The plant is drought resistant and can grow around the Mediterranean. It could have been a reliable source of harmine and harmaline year after year.

Wild rue is very bitter, unpalatable without a sweetener, and the only sweetener that could be used in ancient Greece was honey. The celibate priestesses of the cult of Demeter called "bees" may have had the job of collecting honey, either from the wild or from their own apiary, for use in the *kykeon.*

Unlike opium, wild rue cannot be safely ingested when mixed with alcohol, since a bad, even lethal, drug interaction may occur. This might explain why Demeter refused wine. To prevent nausea and diarrhea from ingesting wild rue, it is advisable to fast for two days before ingesting it, which is what the initiates did.

Peganum harmala contains a deep red dye. Demeter by custom wore purple robes. Hades, Lord of the Underworld, was portrayed with purple hair (Wasson 1978, 58). It is impossible to know if the ancient Greeks distinguished dark red from purple. Could their gods have acquired their purple attributes by ingesting this plant?

The cult of Demeter may have originated in Minoan Crete before 1500 B.C.E. The *Hymn to Demeter* says that she was of Cretan origin. Her daughter Persephone probably was too (cf. Pasiphae, wife of Minos). As argued in Chapter Five the Minoans cultivated the opium poppy and domesticated bees. Whether they knew or not of ergot alkaloids of wild rue is unknown.

If these interpretations are correct, the priestesses of the cult of Demeter dispensed: opium, a narcotic, and the drink called *kykeon*. The latter may have contained ergot sclerotia from *Claviceps paspali*, together with wild rue. Honey may have been used as a sweetener.

The Cult of Dionysos

There was another popular Greek cult which rivaled Christianity: the cult of Dionysos, god of wine. He originated in the second millennium B.C.E. or earlier in Crete. In the eighth century B.C.E. the Hittite chief god, the storm god, was portrayed draped with a live grapevine and carrying a large bunch of grapes (McGovern 2003, 189).

Dionysos also personified the spirit of unfettered youthful Joy. No god or goddess since Dionysos has replaced him. Various monotheistic religious holidays are times of joyous celebration, but they have to offset a heavy sense of guilt, sin, and fear that may afflict some believers most of the year.

Dionysos was a dying-reborn god. The grapevine he represented was deciduous: it lost its leaves in the fall and was dormant over the winter. It brought forth new leaves in the spring. Moreover, in the year 1613 B.C.E., for example, the constellation of Dionysos (Scorpius) would have been "born" in the east at 6 p.m. on May 4; it then disappeared over the western horizon for over four months and was "reborn" on Sept. 24 when it reappeared on the eastern horizon at 8 a.m.

In Greece (but not Minoan Crete) Dionysos was associated with another plant, the ivy (*Hedera helix,* English ivy). The leaves of this plant contain hederin, a glycoside that can cause hallucinations, delirium and stupor (Russell et al. 1997). Today it would be necessary to eat a large amount of the leaves of English ivy to obtain these effects, but in ancient Greece there may have been a more potent variant of this plant. Ivy poisoning by ingestion may have been contributed to the bizarre and violent behavior of the maenads of Dionysos.

According to myth, Dionysos was the son of Zeus, chief of the gods, and of a mortal virgin, Semele (or Persephone). Since Zeus was married to Hera, Dionysos was illegitimate. He reputedly turned water into wine and was said to return from the dead.

The Biblical scholars of the Jesus Seminar do not think the story about Jesus turning water into wine (John 2:1–10) is authentic. It may have been borrowed from one of the Greek communities in first century C.E. Palestine. The notion of a god engendering a son by a mortal virgin was a commonplace in Greek mythology.

Dionysos was connected with the bull and the leopard. The leopard was associated with the pregnant goddess of Çatal Höyük. As suggested in Chapter Two this figure may have been inspired by the starry quadruped, Canis Major, who was under the control of Mistress of Animals. On the Phaistos Disk the Dionysos symbol rose in the east (May 4) on the day before Canis Major and Minor set in the West at dawn.

The week of Carnival, preceding Lent and usually in February, coincided with the Athenian ritual of celebrating the beginning of spring with the opening of jars of matured wine. It was in honor of Dionysos and Hermes. The Athenian event may have inspired the Christian event.

The midwinter holiday of Dionysos on January 9–10 may correspond to January 6, the day of gift-giving and the new year in the eastern Christian churches. Western Christians call it the twelfth day of Christmas or Day of the Three Kings.

Dionysos had a parallel in ancient Egypt. The Egyptians believed that Osiris taught men how to plant grapevines and to make grapes into wine. He was killed by his evil god Seth. The day of the rising of the star Sirius before dawn in Egypt was the time to start the grape harvest and to celebrate the rebirth of Osiris. His rebirth was symbolized by the grapevines which adorned the tombs of Thebes (McGovern 2003, 134–135).

The Timing of Athenian Festivals in the Fifth Century B.C.E.

The timing of the festivals of Demeter and Dionysos in the fifth century B.C.E., the great age of Athens, is vague. We know that these festivals were not correlated with the solstices and equinoxes, with the cycles of the moon, or with the movements of the planets.

The approach used here is to reconstruct the sky of Athens in 422 B.C.E., when timekeeping was fairly careful, and to relate the festivals to the well-known movements of the certain stars and constellations. The program used to reconstruct the sky was *Your Sky*.

It is believed that the Athenian year began after the end of summer heat, the first month being Hekatombian. The beginning of the grape harvest in Athens was timed to the appearance in the east at dawn of the star Protrygeter in the constellation of Virgo (Evans 1998). This was on August 15 in 422 B.C.E.

In Minoan Crete in 1613 B.C.E., as shown in the decipherment of the Phaistos Disk, the probable date for the beginning of the grape harvest was July 23, for Crete was at Latitude 35 South, three degrees lower than that of Athens, Latitude 38 South. Further, the precession of the equinoxes pushed the rise of Dionysos (Scorpius) back by about seventeen days, making it useless as a sign for the Athenians to begin the grape harvest in 422 B.C.E. (The movement of the precession of the equinoxes is counter-clockwise; it serves to push a star date backward from one year to the next.)

In 422 B.C.E. the celebration of the completion of the grape harvest in rural Greece was called the Oschophoria and occurred when Scorpius rose in the east at dawn, on October 21. In Minoan Crete in 1613 B.C.E. the grape harvest was over by September 24.

There was another festival of Demeter called the Thesmophoria toward the end of October. In 422 B.C.E. Virgo was at its peak on October 30 and the first thin crescent of a new moon was shining. This festival, celebrated by women, was concerned with crop fertility. It was believed that crops grew faster when the moon was waxing.

The festival of Anthesteria, dedicated to Dionysos, by tradition is believed to have occurred at the end of February. In Athens at dawn on February 28, 422 C.E., the constellation Scorpius (the Cretan Dionysos) set in the west. This marked the end of the four ritual months dedicated to Dionysos. The people celebrated by opening their wine jugs and having the first drink of the wine harvested the previous summer and fall.

By the end of February in Greece (as in California) new grass had sprouted and spring flowers were in bloom. Rain showers usually continued until early May and there was much farm work to be done, planting catch crops and harvesting. From the second half of May to early September the weather tended to be hot and dry. Apollo, who was associated with light and the sun, was the guardian spirit of this period.

The Cult of Mithras

The cult of Mithras served to produce a sense of one's place in the universe. It was based on a wealth of astronomical observations by Greek scientists. It began in Rome at the end of the first and the beginning of the second century C.E. It flourished between the second and fourth centuries C.E.

The temples of Mithras displayed the zodiac signs, the five known planets (Mercury, Venus, Mars, Jupiter and Saturn) and the sun and moon. The main ritual was a bull sacrifice originally based on the deeds of the hero Mithras. This occurred near the time of the summer solstice, between late July and late August. While priestesses were prominent in the cult of Demeter, only males participated in the cult of Mithras.

This cult was the clearest example of star worship in the ancient world. It relied upon the work of Hipparchus of Nicaea in the second century B.C.E. He compiled the first star catalog. He also discovered the precession of the equinoxes. A cycle of 26,000 years was regarded as necessary for precession. It took 2,160 years to complete a move from one constellation to another.

According to religious historian David Ulansey, the Stoics thought the precession of the equinoxes had religious implications. A newly discovered god was at work, they believed. By causing the end of the previous age of Tauros, this new cosmic force caused a shift to the age of Aries. This force produced cosmic change; it controlled all the stars and planets.

The constellation of Perseus, identified also as Mithras, was located directly above the constellation of Tauros in summer.

In the Mediterranean Basin, this time was the time of harvest, and the beginning of heat and drought. When the harvest was near, the killing of the bull was seen as producing crops of all kinds. The wine symbolized the blood of the bull.

Conclusion

The cults of Demeter and Dionysos, both of which probably date back to the Bronze Age (second millennium B.C.E.), were examples of sophisticated nature worship. The Greeks revered pure springs, high mountains, tall trees, the sun and the moon, but they *worshiped* Demeter, the goddess of grain, opium poppies, and mother love. Others worshiped the god of wine who provided joy. Finally, in the Eleusinian Mysteries, they hoped for a happiness after death that they might have missed in life.

References

"Agape feasts." *The Catholic Encyclopedia*. 1907–1913. New York: Appleton.

Burkert, Walter. 1985. *Greek Religion.* Cambridge, Mass.: Harvard University Press.

Burroughs, William J. 2005. *Climatic Change in Prehistory.* Cambridge: Cambridge University Press.

Cosmopoulos, Michael B. 2003. *Greek Mysteries: The Archaeology and Ritual of Ancient Greek Sacred Cults.* London: Routledge, 2003.

Dethenne, Marcel. 2005. "Dionysos." *Encyclopedia of Religion,* vol. 4, 2356–2360.

Evans, James. 1998. *The History and Practice of Ancient Astronomy.* New York, Oxford University Press.

Ferguson, Everett. 2003. *Backgrounds of Early Christianity*, third ed. Grand Rapids, Michigan: Erdmans Press.

Foley, Helen P., ed. 1994. *The Homeric Hymn to Demeter*. Princeton, Princeton University Press.

Hendriks, Robert G. 2005. "Demeter." *Encyclopedia of Religion,* vol. 4, 2268–2272.

Hoffman, Harry A. tr. 1990. *Hittite Myths.* Atlanta, Scholars Press.

Homer. 2002. *The Odyssey* (tr. Rodney Merrill) Ann Arbor: University of Michigan.

Kerenyi, Karl. 1967. *Eleusis: Archetypical Image of Mother and Daughter*. New York, Pantheon.

McGovern, Patrick. 2003. *Ancient Wine.* Princeton: Princeton University Press, 2003.

McKenna, Terence. 1992. *Food of the Gods.* New York, Bantam.

Russell, Alice B., et al. 1997. "English ivy." Poisonous Plants of North Carolina. Cooperative Extension Service, North Carolina State University, www.ces.ncsu.edu.

Stannard, Jerry. 1999. "The plant called *moly,*" *Herbs and Herbalism in the Middle Ages and Renaissance.* Aldershot, Ashgate U.K.

Stobaeus. *Florilegium.* 4.52.49.

Wasson, R. Gordon. 1968. *Soma: Divine Mushroom of Immortality.* New York: Harcourt.

——— et al. 1968. *Persephone's Quest.* New Haven: Yale University Press.

——— et al. 1978. *The Road to Eleusis.* New York: Harcourt.

Chapter Eight

From Zoroastrianism to Judaism

The Persian influence on religious development in the Middle East was great. Unlike their Greek rivals, the Persians produced a prophet, Zoroaster (Zarathustra), who moralized and reorganized their religion. The Zoroastrian spiritual beings, like those of the Greeks, were humanized. But Zoroaster taught that a single male god was the Divine Ruler of the Universe. He demoted all the other deities to angels and spirits.

This prophet influenced the great Persian ruler, Cyrus the Great (reigned 559–530 B.C.E.). Cyrus founded an empire that extended from the Nile to the Indus, including most of the Middle East and much of Central Asia. It was the largest empire in the world up to that time.

Cyrus is remembered for his religious tolerance and for his decision-making rule: "Diversity in counsel, unity in command." As warriors of his time went, he was a kind ruler, gracious when victorious.

Before Zoroaster, the jurisdiction of the Middle Eastern deities, as described in written records, was limited to the territory of the people who worshipped them. The Jewish Yahweh was no exception. The political character of a god was parochial: he was the god of a certain tribe or ethnic group. Often he was imagined to be the progenitor, the forefather, the earliest ancestor of that group. In some cases he gave his name to the group, such as Hayk, ancestor of the Hayk (Armenians) who lived in Hayastan (Armenia). But the Persian Divine Ruler of the Universe claimed sovereignty over the whole world as known to his worshippers (that is, the Middle East).

The Zoroastrian Belief System

The innovative belief system that began with Zoroaster included the following tenets:

1. The jurisdiction of the one universal god was not coterminous with the territory of a particular ethnic group. Zoroaster's god was claimed to rule everywhere. He had multi-ethnic jurisdiction.

2. All supernatural beings were organized around two figures, that of the Good Being, and that of the Evil Being.

3. A Savior, born of a virgin mother, would come to the spiritual rescue of humanity.

4. Time was not regarded as merely cyclical, following the annual solar cycle, but linear as well. The good people would gain eternal life at the coming end of time. Then the evil people would go to Hell. History was thus a linear, morally significant narrative.

5. The same moral rules should apply to everyone everywhere. The Zoroastrians standardized a moral code for the whole known world. There was one God and one morality as well. Morality and religion were fused. Religion was therefore moralized.

In the past this development has been labeled "ethical monotheism" and credited to the Jews. But Judaism is no more and no less monotheistic than Zoroastrianism: both religions have a powerful Evil Spirit: (Ahriman, Shaitan, Satan, Belial). Both Persians and Jews, like all ethnic groups, had moral codes. The problem was in determining to whom such codes applied. To neighbors? Well, who is one's neighbor?

Zoroastrian ideas existed only as oral traditions until the fifth and sixth centuries C.E., when the first written mentions of his ideas appeared. There are traces of Bronze Age technology in Zoroastrian texts. But given his name (Zarathushtra) which contained the word *shoter*, or camel, Zoroaster probably did not predate the commercial breeding of camels, c. 1200 B.C.E. So he may have lived in Persia around 1000 B.C.E. (Boyce 2001 [1979], 18–9; 1984, 12 and 75; Nigosian 1993, 16 and 30; and Choksy 2005, 9988–99).

Zoroastrian Influence on Judaism

Zoroastrian influence on Judaism probably began after a Jewish catastrophe. In July, 585 B.C.E. Nebuchadnezzar II, ruler of the Babylonian Empire, crushed the small state of Judah and seized Jerusalem. He laid waste to the city and the temple and took many captive Jews back to Mesopotamia. But in 539 Cyrus the Great of Persia defeated Nebuchadezzar II and took over Mesopotamia (Iraq). Even after Cyrus permitted the Jews to return to Palestine in 538 B.C.E., a large Jewish population remained in Mesopotamia. The generosity of Cyrus helped the Jews to believe in a universal God.

The first Persian Empire, 550–332 B.C.E., survived until the conquests of Alexander the Great of Macedon. By then, the use of camels for caravan trade had enabled stronger connections between the inland cities in the arid Middle East, such as Susa (in southwestern Persia), Babylon, Damascus, Aleppo, and Cairo. Better ships and more accurate navigation made possible better marine connections between the great ports of the Mediterranean, the Persian Gulf and the Indian Ocean. As a result of the peace Cyrus established over a wide area, plants, animals, new ideas, and patterns of behavior could spread more easily.

In the fifth century B.C.E., the *magi,* as the Zoroastrian priests were called at the time, revered Nature, although they disliked wild animals, reptiles and insects. This was perhaps a reaction against the zoomorphism present in the ancient kingdoms in the area.

The magi were stargazers who sought to predict the future, a skill that enabled them to make a living wherever they travelled.

Zoroastrian boys at puberty when initiated into the faith were given a sacred cord (*kusti)*, which was tied around their waist (cf. Brahmin initiates, Chapter One). The significance of a cord is that threads which are twisted together to form it are stronger thereby than the same number of strings hanging separately.

In the Hellenistic period, 323 to 30 B.C.E., the Jews and Persians were still in contact in various parts of the Middle East, not only in Persia but also in Asia Minor (Anatolia) as well. Jewish priests, called Zadokites, communicated with Zoroastrian priests, called Magi.

The conquests of Alexander spread the knowledge of Greek over much of the Middle East. It became the common language of the eastern Mediterranean (Nigosian 1993, 97). This was helpful to Persians. Greek and Persian were closely related Indo-European languages. At that time Greek included few Latin words and Persian included few Arabic words.

In the Jewish community of Qumran, (150 B.C.E. to 70 C.E. B.C.E.) the doctrine of the Two Spirits, reflected in the Dead Sea Scrolls, was a striking example of Persian religious influence on the Jews (Hultgard 1999, 39–83; and Philonenko 1995, 163–21).

In the Sassanian imperial period, (226–651 C.E.), Zoroastrianism became influential over an area almost as great at times as the area of the earlier Achaemenian Empire of Cyrus the Great. Zoroastrian priests controlled the schools of Persia. They threatened people with talk of Hell, and promised Paradise for those who were obedient.

Zoroastrianism survived in Persia even after the Muslim Arabs defeated the Sassanians in 642 C.E. and introduced Islam. Many of the adherents of Zoroastrianism, called Perses (Parsees) migrated to Bombay (now Mumbai), where they survive today.

Haoma (Hom), the Zoroastrian Sacred Drink

According to tradition, Zoroaster left his home at the age of twenty and lived in the desert as a hermit. At thirty he received his first vision. During the spring equinox festival it was customary to prepare the sacred *haoma,* so at dawn Zoroaster waded into a certain river to fetch water for the ceremonial drink. Drenched in the current, he entered a purified state. Turning back to shore, he saw a shining being, who took him to the supreme god of the Persians, Ahura Mazda (Ormazd), and five other radiant figures. Zoroaster was so overwhelmed with light he could not see his shadow on the earth. From these beings he received his first revelation: the genesis of the world in seven stages (cf. the seven days of Creation in *Genesis*).

Haoma was probably in use among the Persians and their kin in India long before Zoroaster was born. In India the equivalent word was *soma.* The Hindus worshipped *Soma* as a god.

The nature of this substance has been subject to much speculation. Mott T. Green (1992) argued that the source of *haoma* was the microfungus of the Claviceps family. *Claviceps paspali* colonizes a wide variety of wild grasses. Like *haoma,* this fungus has no leaves, flowers, or seeds. Like *haoma,* it grows in the moist cool areas in the *mountains* of the Middle East. The ancient Persian priests praised the clouds and rain that helped *haoma* to grow in the heights of mountains and abysses between them. The cold mountain winters also provided the sharp drop to freezing and below in winter temperature, which must last at last 25 days for the maturation of the fungal spores. In the mountains the fungus undergoes long exposure to ultraviolet light, which serves to concentrate certain alkaloids.

Haoma was produced by pounding and crushing its "stems." The stems of grass colonized by *Claviceps paspali* contain lines of globular adhesions. The little globes are the sclerotia of the fungus, which contain the hallucinogenic alkaloids. The honeydew produced by the fungus was sweet smelling, as was *haoma* (Greene 1992, 106–138; Boyce 1984, 52, 56 and 73–74). The "pressing" of the *haoma* may have referred not only the use of mortar and pestle, but also have referred to the pressure used on teats to obtain the contaminated milk from the udder of cows, mares, ewes, and nanny goats that had grazed on the colonized grass.

The Geographical Context, Persia and Palestine

Most Persians lived in the northern and western highlands (the Alborz and Zagros Mountains). In these areas there were sufficient grasslands to support herds of horses, cattle, sheep, and goats. Today 27% of the land in Iran consists of permanent pastures. Moreover, the melting snows and sub-freezing December and January temperatures in these areas make possible the widespread *Claviceps paspali* colonization of grasses. The continental climate of the highlands was similar to that of the Ukrainian steppe, from which the Persian tribes had come.

In the midst of the Alborz Mountains, 41 miles from Tehran, stands a volcanic peak, Mt. Damavand, at 5,671 meters (18,601 feet) the highest peak in the Middle East. Its fumaroles produce sulfur. When Mt. Damavand was a more active volcano, it may have been the original model for Hell.

In contrast, Egypt, Mesopotamia, and the Levant had very limited land for grazing. Their climate was like that of California, Mediterranean rather than continental. Only a few areas, like Galilee, had abundant rainfall and were well suited to grazing animals.

The only time when a significant amount of fungal colonization occurred in the grassy areas was in spring *when rainfall was abundant*. So there was not only a place, but a time factor involved in finding the ingredients for *haoma*.

Espand (*Esfand*, Wild Rue)

Other plant ingredients may have been added to the *haoma* mixture. One is *Peganum harmala* (wild rue). It contains harmine and harmaline, which are the richest source of MAOI (monoamine oxidase inhibitors). These are synergic with the hallucinogenic ergot alkaloids, enhancing the latter's potency by inhibiting the re-uptake of serotonin by the neurons of the brain (Al-Shamma et al., 1981, 745–747).

Espand (*esfand*), as the Persians call wild rue, is commonly burned as incense at weddings and widely used to protect against the Evil Eye. Wild rue was so important in ancient Persian culture that the last month of the year was named for it. The month of *Esfand* lasts from February 20 to March 20. The old Persian year began at the spring equinox, March 21 (Noruz).

The Persians called the *espand* plant "holy." In Zoroastrianism there is a benevolent female figure, Spenta Armaita (in Armenia, Spendaramet). Spent = holy; Aram = serene, calm. This probably refers to the mood of calm elation that the ingestion of an extract from the *espand* plant can produce.

The alkaloid-bearing seeds of *espand* appear in semi-arid land in the late summer or early fall. They can be dried and preserved, and then prepared in the month of *Espand* for ritual use at the Noruz Festival, which lasts for thirteen days. The peak in the colonization of ergot alkaloids on wild grasses and cereals may come about this time if the weather is favorable. However, the peak in fungal colonization of grass may come later in spring.

Harry Falk has argued that extracts from a species of the genus ephedra, which is used today by the Parsees (Zoroastrians of India), served to replace ergot (Falk 1989). But ephedra species have leaves. They flourish in dry climates. They contain ephedrine, which raises blood pressure. They are not hallucinogenic, and so they cannot account for the visions of Zoroaster and his priests.

To obtain the hallucinogenic *Claviceps paspali,* the Parsees of Mumbai would have had to travel up into the Himalayas and find a meadow frozen for at least 25 days in winter. Then they would have had to convey the fungally colonized grass rapidly down to steaming Bombay and use it immediately. No wonder they were content with ephedra.

The Political Usefulness of Zoroastrianism

Much of the weight of responsibility for everything that happened in a state or empire could be shifted from the shoulders of the king to the Deity. When the king was unable or unwilling to fulfill the wishes of the people, he could appeal to the invisible Good Deity or blame the equally invisible Evil Deity.

The "divinely inspired" moral rules could be used to settle conflicts between peoples with different moral rules and customs. Moreover, those rules were endorsed not just by a tribal god, or a storm god, or even a king, but by no less than the Divine Ruler of the Universe. When it appeared that some individual or group was breaking the rules, the rulers could threaten them with *eternal* punishment.

When morality was legitimized as the Will of God, any attack on God could be interpreted as an attack on morality. Any attack on morality, which was necessary for the survival of society, was felt to be an attack on society. That is why atheists through the centuries have been seen as dangerous traitors, as threats to the security of everyone. The sanctification of morality was a basic defense of the new belief system. It was believed to protect society against any outbreaks of doubt in the beneficence of the rulers.

Judaism

So why did the Jews reimagine their tribal god as the Divine Ruler of the Universe? The Jews were few in number and they did not rule an empire. Horse-related technologies were essential for all armies after 750 B.C.E., but the Jews lacked the money and pasture to support large herds of warhorses. They could not aspire to building an independent state as long as they fought only on foot.

Thus they were attracted to the idea of a universal god to redeem them in a Last Judgment.

The Jews had another reason for accepting a Divine Ruler of the Universe. The experience of deportation and exile influenced them to look for a god who would take care of them wherever they were. The Jews needed a portable god, one who was just and merciful in the midst of an unjust world far from Palestine. The portable god could not be an image or a figure: Moses had forbidden it. So the Jews imagined an invisible, omnipresent God who did not need to be carried from place to place. They were even forbidden to write his name. Ingenious!

After the Romans deported the Jews from Palestine (71 C.E.) and Christians spread their religion in the eastern Mediterranean, the Jews and Christians imagined a new natural background for religion. As has been shown, from prehistoric times, many deities had been linked with animals, planets, and constellations of stars. With the shift to "monotheism" it was no longer possible to identify the Supreme Ruler with an animal, planet, or group of stars. He—it was always a "He"—was conceived to live in Heaven: up in the sky. God was said to control the movements of the sun, moon, stars and "willful" planets. To support Him in Heaven there were angels, archangels, cherubim, and seraphim, falling down before Him—a complete team of worshipful servants. God had moral jurisdiction over everyone. So the Jews could not lose him by moving around; nor could the enemies of the Jews escape His punishment.

The Divine Ruler of the Universe had the personality of a Lord of lords. God was given to anger, but his priests said that He had the best interests of the people at heart.

The tribal customary laws of the Jews and other societies of the Middle East were edited and molded by the priests who claimed to speak for the Divine Ruler. They claimed that the moral rules they made, expressing the Divine Will, were superior to tribal laws.

Priests and scribes put these rules into writing. Unlike a king, who might be capricious and arbitrary, the Divine Ruler of the Universe let people know just where He stood. Since women were excluded from the codification and sanctification of laws, they did not fare well in the new legal system.

As time went on, the "spirit world" in the Middle East was both expanded and contracted. It was expanded by syncretism, the combination of different forms of religious belief and practice. "Pagan" holidays could be converted into monotheistic holidays by sprinkling a little holy water over them. "Pagan" goddesses, decently clothed, could be converted into saints. "Pagan" temples could be torn down and synagogues, churches, or mosques could be built on the same sites.

But if a people became disenchanted with their rulers and establishment priests, they could create new sects and denominations, each with its territorial holdings, thus contracting the sacred territory in the hands of their rulers. Such religious dissidents, of course, were a threat to the established religion and the state, and therefore might be persecuted.

By the time of Jesus, in the thinking imported from Persia, the Ruler of the Universe was strongly associated with Light—or brightness, radiance, shining, etc. Light was God's most important symbol.

Light Symbolism in the Hebrew Bible

Unmistakable light symbolism may be found in only two books of the Hebrew Bible: Ezekiel and Daniel. Both may have contained material written during the period of Persian dominance (538–330) in the Middle East, or later when Persian influence spread by means of an expanding Armenian state. Parts of the book of Daniel may have been written in the late second century B.C.E. The passages are:

> As I looked, a stormy wind came out of the north: a great cloud with brightness around it and fire flashing forth continually, and in the middle of the fire, something like gleaming amber (Ezekiel 1:4, NRSV).

Ezekiel heard a loud rumbling sound coming from the fire and interpreted it as the voice of the Lord. Daniel had a dream and saw visions while lying in bed.

> As I watched, thrones were set in place, and an Ancient One took his throne, his clothing was white as snow, and the hair of his head like pure wool; his throne was fiery flames, and its wheels were burning fire. A stream of fire issued and flowed out from his presence (Daniel 7: 9–10, NRSV).

These passages suggest that Ezekiel and Daniel had some experience with the hallucinogen used by the Zoroastrian priests.

Beginning in 400 B.C.E. the weather in the eastern Mediterranean grew warm and entered a wet phase (see Chapter Nine). There were no new mass invasions from the steppes and the deserts. The times were improving.

After 31 B.C.E. the well-organized Roman Empire was able to keep order within and hold the Celts, Germans and other "barbarians" at bay. In this time of greater prosperity and security it may be that the people became less afraid and more hopeful. This was the atmosphere in which Christianity emerged.

Conclusion

Zoroaster fused morality and religion into a unified belief system with universal applications. He viewed History as a single, morally significant narrative. He also created a symbolism of Light, very likely inspired by experiences with a hallucinogen.

As a result of the conquests of Cyrus II and others, and new transportation technologies, Zoroastrianism spread. It probably influenced the Jews after their exile in the sixth century B.C.E. The geography of Persia favored the growth of the two ingredients needed to make a hallucinogenic drink. Persian conquests and new technologies of transport served to spread these ideas among the Jews.

Zoroastrian ideas were useful not only for established rulers and priests, but also for dissenters. The Jews found such ideas suited to the needs of their diaspora.

References

Ahmadzai, Hangama. 2005. "If looks could kill: The story of the evil eye." The Roashans, roashan.com.

Al Shamma, et al. 1981. "Anti-microbial agents for higher plants." *Journal of Natural Products* 44:6, 745–747.

Boyce, Mary, ed. and tr. 1984. *Textual Sources for the Study of Zoroastrianism.* Chicago: University of Chicago Press.

———. 2001 [1979]. *Zoroastrians: Their Religious Beliefs and Practices.* New York: Routledge.

Bulliet, Richard W. 1990. *The Camel and the Wheel.* New York: Columbia University Press.

Choksy, Jamsheed K. 2005. "Zoroastrianism." *Encyclopedia of Religion*, Second ed., vol. 14, 9988–10008.

Coogan, Michael D., ed. 2001. *The New Oxford Annotated Bible.* Third ed., The New Revised Standard Edition. Oxford: Oxford University Press.

Falk, Harry. 1989. "Soma I and II." *Bulletin of the School of Oriental and African Studies*. 52(1). 77–90.

Flattery, David. 1989. *Haoma and Harmaline*. Berkeley: University of California Press.

Gracie and Zarkov. 1986. "Peganum harmala: An Indo-European plant teacher." Erowid Vault, erowid.org.

Greene, Mott T. 1992. *Natural Knowledge in Pre-Classical Antiquity*. Baltimore: Johns Hopkins.

Hultgard, Anders. 1999. "Persian Apocalyptism." *The Encyclopedia of Apocalyptism*. Ed. John J. Collins. New York: Continuum. 39–83.

Iran Chamber Society. n.d. "The early years of Sassanid Empire and religious turmoil in Persia." Iran Chamber Society, www.iranchamber.com.

Issar, Arie S., and Mattanyah Zohar. 2004. *Climate Change: Environment and Civilization in the Middle East*. Berlin: Springer.

Jay, Mike. 1999. *Blue Tide, The Search for Soma*. Brooklyn, N.Y.: Autonomedia.

Křen, Vladimír, and Ladislav Cvak. 1999. *Ergot: The Genus Claviceps*. London: CRC Press.

Nigosian, S.A. 1993. *The Zoroastrian Faith*. Montreal: McGill-Queens University Press.

"Peganum harmala." Erowid Vault, erowid.org.

Most, Albert. 1985. *Peganum Harmala: The Hallucinogenic Herb of the American Southwest* (Denton, Texas: Venom Press). Erowid.org.

"Pentacle." Wikipedia.

Peters, F. E. 2003. *The Monotheists*. Vol. 2 Princeton: Princeton University Press.

Philonenko, M. 1995. "La doctrine qoumranienne des Deux Esprits: Ses origines iraniennes et ses prolongements dans le judaisme essenien et la Christianisme antique." *Apocalyptique iranienne et dualisme qoumranien.* G. Widengren et al., eds. Paris: Maisonneuve. 163–212.

Rudgley, Richard. 2000. *The Encyclopedia of Psychoactive Substances.* New York: St. Martin's Press.

"The Sassanid Empire." Wikipedia.

Scarborough, John. 1996. "The opium poppy in Hellenistic and Roman medicine." *Drugs and Narcotics in History.* Roy Porter and Mikulas Tech, eds. Cambridge: Cambridge University Press.

Vermes, Geza. 2004. *The Complete Dead Sea Scrolls in English*. Rev. ed. London: Penguin.

Winkelman, Michael. 2000. *Shamanism: The Neural Ecology of Consciousness and Healing.* Westport, Conn.: Bergen and Garvey.

Chapter Nine

Visions and the Origins of Christianity

Introduction

In 2006 Ronald R. Griffiths and his team at Johns Hopkins University demonstrated in a double-blind experiment that the hallucinogen psilocybin, extracted from a mushroom, could induce a mystical experience. They chose 36 participants, all but one of them college graduates, who at least intermittently had participated in religious and spiritual activities. After two months, two-thirds of the participants reported that ingesting psilocybin had been a complete "mystical" experience: one of the five most meaningful, even *the* most meaningful, of their lives (Griffiths 2006, 268–283. See also Borg et al. 2003).

The above experiment started with a cause (a hallucinogen) and reported its effects (a mystical experience). To accurately infer causes from effects is more difficult. Constructing a single causal narrative from concurrent facts is riskier still, often leading to the production of a charming but mistaken myth.

People tend to perceive more clearly those facts that appear to confirm their beliefs, rather than facts that contradict them. Yet, time and time again, scientists have discovered that the discrepant fact turns out to be the key to solving a problem. This chapter will examine discrepant material in the New Testament.

The four canonical Christian Gospels are like four gardens containing weeds: that is, discrepant facts and episodes that the gardeners failed to uproot or to fully harmonize with their message. The Gospel writers treated the weeds as miraculous and used them as proof of the divine nature of Jesus, yet they had nothing to do with his moral teachings.

The Jesus Seminar color-coded the text according to the probable authenticity of each passage; that is, as an expression of what Jesus "really" meant (Funk et al. 1993). Discrepant passages were coded as grey or black, while "authentic" material was coded as red or pink. The Seminarians assumed that the "real" Jesus was primarily a moral teacher. However, they did not take into consideration the *physical* environment in which he lived.

Another way to approach the Gospels is to take heed of the scientific experiment described above. Evidently, many people can have profound religious experiences when under the influence of a hallucinogen. Hallucinogens can be extracted from plants and fungi. Could these facts be of any use in understanding the "weeds" in the Gospels? Could they lead to a more accurate reconstruction of the origins of Christianity? Let us see.

A vision may be chemically induced, as shown by the above experiment. How can one decide whether a vision is chemically induced or not? Some visions are connected with sleep; others are produced consciously by the imagination; and still others result from mental illness. But the effects induced by a hallucinogen always have a marker: at some point: *they involve characteristic distortions in visual perception.*

Ronald Siegel and M. E. Jarvik reported that hallucinogens in general cause a bright light to appear in the center of the energy field of the subject (Siegel and Jarvik 1975, 115). They may cause auditory hallucinations and high anxiety as well (Alatrash et al. 2006, 550–551; Satora et al. 2005, 394–396; Dobkin de Rios 2003, 43–44). Hallucinogens may cause transient blindness (Pootanakit 2001, 77–85; Cherian 2005, 938–939).

There are no statements in the Bible to the effect that any individual ingested a hallucinogen. But this silence is not strange. The Greek priestesses in ancient Eleusis served a sacred drink, *kykeon*. They kept its recipe secret for centuries. Scholars still argue about the content of the *kykeon* recipe, but they generally agree it contained a hallucinogen (Valencic 1994). If a sacred drink is beneficial, those with a monopoly of knowledge about its preparation possess an advantage over their competitors. Such knowledge is like an old family recipe or a trade secret.

Given the nature of the Biblical texts, which have been copied and re-copied, cut and pasted, scholars know that these texts cannot be taken at face value. Many people no longer believe that the Bible contains only literal truth uttered by a Supreme Being, because such a Being would not have changed His mind hundreds of times (Ehrman 2005, passim). Moreover, if any of the component books in the Bible ever contained any recipes for a hallucinogen, an editor would likely have deleted them, since they might have undermined the legitimacy of the message he wished to send.

In the New Testament the only sacred drink mentioned is wine, which Jesus and his disciples, like other Jews, drank. Too much wine, however, does not produce spiritual experiences and lasting peace of mind, but a headache. Perhaps on occasion Jesus and his disciples made use of a more suitable drink, one that lifted their spirits instead of giving a nasty hangover. If so, how could it be detected?

1. The probable ingredients would have to be identified.

2. It would be necessary to show that those ingredients were available in first-century Palestine.

3. It would be necessary to identify extraordinary experiences of Jesus and his followers that might have been induced by such a drink. Then it would be necessary to make a differential diagnosis of these extraordinary experiences.

Visual and Auditory Disturbances in the New Testament

1. The episode of the transfiguration of Jesus is found in Matthew 17:1–9, Mark 9:2, and Luke 9:29. Jesus took three disciples, Peter, James, and John, to the top of a mountain. According to Matthew:

> And he [Jesus] was transfigured before them and his face shone like the sun, and his clothes became dazzling white. Suddenly there appeared to them Moses and Elijah talking with him.... Suddenly a bright cloud overshadowed them and a voice said, "This is my Son, The Beloved, with him I am well pleased; listen to him." When the disciples heard this they fell to the ground and were overcome with fear.
>
> But Jesus came and touched them saying, "Get up and do not be afraid." And when they looked up, they saw no one except Jesus himself alone. As they were coming down the mountain Jesus ordered them,
>
> "Tell no one about the vision until the Son of Man has been raised from the dead."

Differential diagnosis: Migraine headaches may produce visual and auditory hallucinations. So may temporal lobe epilepsy. However, it is improbable that three men would suffer the acute symptoms of such disorders simultaneously. A hallucinogen could have produced the effects reported in the Gospels simultaneously in a group of individuals.

2. A hallucinogen may also be suspected as a cause of the vision of Paul of Tarsus: (Acts 9:3–4):

> As Paul was approaching Damascus, "suddenly a light from Heaven flashed around him. He fell to the ground and heard a voice saying to him, 'Saul, Saul, why do you persecute me?'" For three days Paul was blinded.

Differential diagnosis: as suggested by Kenneth Dewhurst et al., Paul could have suffered an attack of temporal lobe epilepsy. However, transient blindness has only been reported in cases of occipital lobe epilepsy. The vision center of the brain is in the occipital lobe. Migraine headaches may cause transient blindness, but only in one eye. However, all the effects reported by Paul could have been chemically induced.

There is other evidence for chemical induction of mental phenomena. The next two sections of this article are discussions of two thought patterns prevalent in Palestine in the time of Jesus.

Light as a Symbol

The use of light in general as a symbol of divinity is especially prominent in the Gospel of John:

> What has come into being in him was life, and the life was light of all people. The light shines in the darkness and the darkness did not overcome it.
>
> There was a man sent from God whose name was John. He came as a witness to testify to the light, so that all might believe through him. He himself was not the light, but he came to testify to the light. The true light, which enlightens everyone, was coming into the world (John 1:3–9).

In John 8:12, Jesus says "I am the light of the world. Whoever follows me will not walk in darkness but will have the light of life."

The beginning of Revelation blazes with light:

> And in the midst of the lamp stands I saw one like the Son of Man, clothed with a long robe and with a golden sash around his chest. His head and his hair were white as white wool, white as snow; his eyes like aflame of fire, his feet like

> burnished bronze, refined as in a furnace....his face was like the sun shining with full force (1:13–16).

But light has not always been a symbol of goodness in the Middle East. Before the sixth century B.C.E. (i.e. before the common era or BC) the sun was worshipped in Egypt and elsewhere in the Middle East, but light and darkness had no ethical associations. They were seen as complementary phenomena, not irreconcilable opposites (Werblavsky 2005, 5450–5455).

The Middle Eastern summer is much hotter and drier than that of northwestern Europe. The sun can be a killer. People often choose to travel at night across desert areas, welcoming the cooler air and the brilliant starlight. There is usually no rain from late spring to early fall in the lands around the Mediterranean Sea. Rain and clouds are welcomed more than sunlight, which is abundant. Recall that the chief male god in ancient Greece, Anatolia, and the Levant was a thunder god, the bringer of rain.

In about the sixth century B.C.E., light began to take on moral significance, representing goodness and wisdom, in Middle Eastern thinking. The experience of Zoroaster (Zarathushtra, Zardusht), whom some experts believe lived at this time, may be cited again.

When Zoroaster was 30 years old, at the time of the spring equinox festival, he went to a river and waded into the water until midstream. When he turned around to wade back he saw a divine being "in the shape of a man, fair, bright, and radiant. ... He wore a garment of silk ... which was as light itself." The shining figure took Zoroaster to a group of divine beings who gave off so much light that he could no longer see his shadow on the ground (Boyce 1984, 75).

Light as a symbol of goodness would have made sense to people who had experienced brilliant light in connection with blissful feelings while in a trance.

Zoroaster taught that the chief god in his religion, Ahura Mazda, lived in a place of "Endless Light." This god created fire and linked its brilliance to Endless Light. The Zoroastrians were often called "fire worshippers," but in fact fire was only a symbol of their chief god.

Many centuries later, in 1652, George Fox, the founder of the Quakers, reported in his journal while at an inn near Pendle Hill, in northwest England: "Here the Lord opened unto me, and let me see a great people in white raiment by the river side, coming to the Lord" (Fox 1911, I, 40). The first mention of light as a symbol of goodness appeared in Fox's diary in 1648; the last appeared ten years later. Fox died in 1691.

Trembling and other central nervous symptoms among the Quakers between 1647 and 1659 may have been caused by the unintended presence of ergot alkaloids in the rye bread in the diet of English commoners (Matossian 2007). In this period, the climate in England shifted from maritime to continental, favoring the formation of ergot alkaloids. But long after 1659, and even today, Quakers use light as a symbol to suggest the love of God and Jesus.

The Early History of Apocalyptic Thinking

Apocalyptic thinking pervades the New Testament. It is concerned with the end of the world, the afterlife, the last judgment of the dead, a savior, and a new age. The first gospel to be written was probably the Gospel of Mark, tentatively dated at 65 C.E. (the common era, or A.D.). It indicates that Jesus believed that the end of the world was not only inevitable but *imminent*.

> Truly I tell you, there are some standing here who will not taste of death until the Kingdom of Heaven has come with power (Mark 9:1: see also Matt. 16:28).

> Truly I tell you, this generation will not pass away until all these things have taken place (Mark 13:30, see also Luke 21:32).

Apocalyptic beliefs were important in the Christian message because they supported the view that Jesus had the supernatural power of prophecy and was the expected savior. Such beliefs were held by John the Baptist and the disciples of Jesus (Allison 1999, 267–302).

But the end of the world did not arrive on schedule, within a generation. This called into question the claim of early Christians that Jesus was a prophet and savior. So Matthew (writing in 90–110 C.E., two generations after the death of Jesus) attributed to Jesus the saying that only the Father knows the actual date of the end of the world (24:36). Luke, writing one or two generations after the death of Jesus) said that the Kingdom of Heaven had already arrived (11:20 and 17:20–21).

Apocalyptic thinking was part of the climate of opinion of the Jews in the first century C.E. But the Jews had not always believed in the end of the world and the coming of a Savior. Apocalyptic thinking had Middle Eastern and Greek sources but the most important were Persian.

In the time of Cyrus the Great, 550–530 B.C.E., apocalyptic and dualistic thinking had been integrated into Persian culture (Strausberg 2008, 105–110).

The Persians continued to dominate the Middle East until 332 C.E., when the Greeks replaced them. In the second century the Parthians took over Persia and Mesopotamia and perpetuated Zoroastrian religious influence in the area until 77 B.C.E. So did the neighboring Armenians, who were strongly influenced by Zoroastrianism (Russell 1987).

Apocalyptic thinking focuses not on religious traditions but on the current and future work of supposed supernatural powers. At this time the struggle between good and evil powers was seen in the rise and fall of nations ("historical" apocalyptism). The judgment of the dead, and their consignment to Heaven or Hell, would occur on a single day. The forces of the good Divine Ruler would defeat the forces of the Evil Spirit, as yet unidentified.

In the third century B.C.E., this historical apocalyptic thinking appeared among the Jews, becoming a "cultural epidemic." It lasted until the early second century C.E. among Jews and Christians (Allison 1999, 267–302).

The Roman Empire was prospering in the first and second centuries C.E. Climatic conditions were favorable. The subject populations probably grew, producing more tax revenues. In return the Romans were delivering many important benefits to their subjects: security from barbarian attacks, a flourishing agricultural economy, well-protected trade routes by land and sea, and a uniform system of law and justice. As Dale Allison admits, in the time of Jesus there was no particular political or social crisis to produce a receptive audience for apocalyptic thinking (Allison 1999, 299). On the contrary, there was reason for optimism.

Was apocalyptism a result of Roman oppression of the Jews? One could explain the *decline* of apocalyptism that way. After Jewish revolts against Rome failed in the first and early second centuries C.E., apocalyptic thinking died down. Those who believed the apocalyptic prophecies may have been disillusioned by the failure of Jewish rebels. But that explains neither the previous *emergence* of widespread Jewish apocalyptic thinking in the relatively free and prosperous Hellenistic period nor its continuance during the centuries of peak Roman prosperity and stability.

There are some remarkable similarities between light symbolism and apocalyptic thinking, on the one hand, and on the other, the mental effects of LSD (lysergic acid diethylamide) on volunteers in the United States between 1952 and 1972. These similarities suggest that the hallucinations of hippies and the "glory" in the gospels might have had a similar origin.

Hallucinations and Recent Religious Experience

The hallucinogen LSD-25—lysergic acid diethylamide—can produce visual and auditory hallucinations, apocalyptic visions, and "mystical" experiences.

This chemical was created and recognized as a powerful hallucinogen by a Swiss chemist, Dr. Albert Hofmann in the Sandoz Laboratory in 1943 (Novartis today). But it is a derivative of a group of natural chemicals found in ergot, a product of the fungus *Claviceps purpurea* and *Claviceps paspali.* Tens of thousands of Americans, perhaps hundreds of thousands, have ingested LSD, legally and illegally. Illegal LSD use continues today (Henderson, 1994, 3; Dobkin de Rios, 2003, x; and Schiff 2006, 98).

The nature of LSD experiences depends heavily on two factors: set and setting. If the mood and expectations of the subject (the set) are positive; and the setting for his experience is supportive, the subject is likely to have a pleasant experience, "a good trip." If the subject is isolated, harassed, or has an anxious or resentful mood, or if he is suffering from mental or physical illness, he is more likely to have an unpleasant experience, or "bummer." For a good trip, the subject must be guided by a sympathetic person knowledgeable about LSD (Lee 1985, 58).

Reports of LSD experiences usually include visual disturbances. Timothy Leary described his first LSD experience, fall 1961:

> Tumbling and spinning, down the soft fibrous avenues to some central point which was just light, just light, but not just light: It was the Center of Life. A burning, dazzling,

> throbbing radiant core, pure pulsing exulting light (Leary 1968, 246).

In an experience during the winter of 1961 he reported:

> The room was celestial, glowing radiant illumination … light … light … light … The people present were transfigured.… Godlike creatures.… Gradually the brilliant illumination faded back to the Three-D world and I sat up. Reborn, Renewed, Radiant with affection and reverence.

In an apocalyptic experience, Leary saw a fantastic battle between Light and Darkness, occurring at all levels of being. Afterwards he said:

> I found myself in a rather unusual state of mind; I felt a mixture of serenity and bliss with the naïve primitive faith of the early Christians: It was a world where miracles were possible, acceptable, and understandable" (O'Leary 1968, 246).

Bernard Aronson reported that early in an LSD experience he viewed the world as a battleground between the "Children of Light and the Children of Darkness," and that he identified with the former (Aronson 1970, 45).

Between 1956 and 1962, a physician, Dr. Oscar Janiger, did research on the effects of LSD by prescribing it to a total of 930 adult volunteers. He selected only volunteers who showed no sign of significant mental or physical illness. Then he provided them with a moderate dose of LSD in a secular, homelike environment with the company of a responsible guide and observer.

His volunteers typically reported visual hallucinations and frequently auditory hallucinations as well. Of the 930 volunteers, 223, or one-fifth, had mystic or spiritual experiences. Notably, one woman imagined herself moving up into "the light."

> I entered the light. A white light, not yellow like fire, or lamplight, or sunlight. As I entered more and more it seemed to pin me, permeate me, through every cell. I was aware of it entering every part of me. This feeling of being surrounded and penetrated by Light lasted for what appeared to be a long, wonderfully long time. I was perfectly relaxed in body, and I felt indescribable joy, something even much stronger. I became one with the light. I was the Light (Dobkin de Rios 2003, 134).

It can be argued that by long spiritual training, hallucinations and feelings of bliss can be produced without the use of psychoactive chemicals. The methods include sensory deprivation, fasting, drumming, chanting, dancing, meditation, yoga exercises, et al. *But the New Testament does not report that the early Christians practiced such spiritual exercises.* Jesus told them stories and performed "miracles." They went to hear him and followed him around. The Gospel reader is expected to believe that supernatural forces produced the extraordinary experiences reported by these followers.

Supernatural beings and supernatural events seen during a religious experience seem undeniably real to the subject. Some think they have experienced "ultimate reality" (Pahnke 1969, 155). Hence, the hallucinatory experience can produce conviction, belief, and lasting faith in supernatural realities.

If a hallucinogen is suspected of creating some of the visions in the New Testament, then what might it be? Therein lies a real mystery.

The Missing Middle East Hallucinogen

In the Middle East from the Neolithic period on, people enjoyed the use of psychoactive substances: beer, wine, opium and hashish. But it is widely believed that no useful hallucinogenic plants grew in the

Fertile Crescent. The datura plant grew there, but it was toxic enough to send the user on a one-way trip to the spirit world.

As for fungi, the usual climate in most of the Middle East was often too dry to encourage their growth. In addition, the staple cereal crops of the Middle East, wheat and barley, were not hospitable to the spores of the ergot fungus *Claviceps purpurea,* because the flowers of these cereals usually remained closed. Ergot rarely colonized any cereal except rye, with its open flowers. As far as is known, little rye was grown in the Middle East in the first century C.E.

In the search for the recipe for *kykeon*, investigators have turned to possible ergot hosts other than cereals. In 1978 Albert Hoffman, the Swiss chemist who discovered the effects of LSD, proposed that hallucinogenic alkaloids might have become available when the fungus *Claviceps paspali,* colonized a ubiquitous Mediterranean wild grass, *Paspalium distichum,* or some other wild grass. LSD can be produced from the ergot alkaloids produced by *Claviceps paspali* (Arcamone 1960, 238–239). Today there are reports of *Claviceps paspali* colonizing various grasses in Iran, Turkey, Italy—and Israel (CAB International 1984).

The appearance of a natural hallucinogen has not been suspected in the arid flatlands and hills of Palestine. However, Jesus lived in a time of favorable climatic conditions in Palestine: indeed, *moisture was at a peak.* Apocalyptic thinking coincided with the beginning of this moist period and died out in the third century C.E. when the climate was becoming more arid (Enzel 2003, 263–273, and Goldreich 2003, 160).

Furthermore, *Galilee*, the home of Jesus, has a *higher rainfall* (c. 900–1200 mm. a year) than the rest of Palestine (Goldreich, 2003, 15). Here one finds Mt. Meron, at 3,955 feet the highest peak in the area. The ergots of *Claviceps paspali* are more likely to appear in the mountains of Galilee than in any other place in Palestine.

Shepherds living on the slopes of the mountains of Galilee may have known that in the spring the milk produced by their flocks had "magical" power. This would explain the appearance of the shepherds in the birth story (Luke 2: 8–18). The shepherds were "keeping watch over their flocks by night. Then the Angel of the Lord stood before them, and the glory of the Lord shown around them, and they were terrified."

Here we find evidence of a possible drug-induced hallucination: brilliant light at night, central focus of light, feeling of fear but a whole group. Why did the vision come to shepherds? Perhaps these shepherds had consumed the freshly contaminated milk produced by their flocks. Perhaps shepherds were the ones who told Jesus the secret.

In addition, some Greeks may have known the secret recipe for *kykeon,* a hallucinogenic drink used in the cult of Demeter in Eleusis. Jesus may have met them in Sepphoris, a Greek trading center just five miles from Nazareth, about an hour's walk.

In the first century C.E. Greeks and Romans commonly used psychoactive drugs for non-medical purposes. In a recent study, D.C.A. Hillman argued that the Greeks and Romans regarded drugs as plants and plant parts, neither good nor bad. They were used for recreation; and some were "no less powerful than most modern street drugs."

The ancient Greeks and Romans saw nothing wrong in using drugs to induce visions. So did other ancients in order to experience what they believed to be the spirit world. They used drugs in their search for divine inspiration, treating them as a "chemical muse."

The Greek cult of Demeter in Roma times attracted thousands to Eleusis where the priestesses were serving *kykeon.* Most investigators think this drink was hallucinogenic.

Greek towns had a cosmopolitan population. The Persians may have been represented in Sepphoris by Zoroastrian priests, whom the Greeks called *magi* (often translated as "wise men"). Those in Matthew 2:1–12 were "from the East." This probably referred to Persia. They may have been telling fortunes by the stars, a common practice of such priests. The Magi used a drug when they wished to "call up the gods" (Hillman 2008, 60–61, 137, and 216–21).

Matthew 2:1–2, 10 says that three *magi* revered Jesus as a newborn baby. But perhaps the contact came later, when Jesus was an adult. Then the reported gifts of the magi would have made better sense. The gold would have served to buy food and clothing for Jesus and his disciples as they went about preaching the gospel. The smoke of frankincense resin is not merely pleasant: research in 2008 showed it to be psychoactive, relieving depression and anxiety. Myrrh, another fragrant resin, was an ingredient in oil used in oil to anoint a king.

Persian influence may have reached Palestine under Roman rule by way of Armenia, a buffer state between the Parthian and Roman empires. In the reign of Tigranes (the Great) 95–55 B.C.E., Armenia had jurisdiction over Syria and Lebanon, up to the border of Judaea. It remained a buffer state during the life of Jesus (Garsoïan 1997, 37–62).

So there were many possible people—shepherds, Greeks, magi, Zoroastrian Armenians—who might have told Jesus the recipe for a hallucinogenic drink.

The Missing Middle East Potentiator

But the solution to the mystery of the missing hallucinogen is not complete. Even if collectors at Eleusis had meadows full of colonized grasses, they might not have been able to find enough ergots to provide for thousands of celebrants. The ergot harvest would have depended on the spring rainfall, which varied from year to year (Peter Webster, n.d., "The secret of the *Kykeon*"). But the priestesses of Demeter and the magi knew of a potentiator, or booster, that could increase the strength of a hallucinogenic drink and the number of effective doses that could be made from it.

Confirmation may be found in the recipe for the famous South American psychedelic drink, *ayahuasca.* This drink has at least two psychoactive ingredients: harmaline, from the plant *Banisteropsis caapi,* and DMT, or dimethyltryptamine, from *Psychotria viridis* and other South American plants. *Ayahuasca* achieves its effect by the synergy of its two main ingredients. Harmaline is a beta-carboline indole alkaloid, and taken alone it can serve as anti-depressant, creating a state of calm elation. DMT is a hallucinogen, stimulating the release of serotonin in the synapses. The beta-carbolines, by inhibiting the output of monoamine oxidase inhibitors, may decrease the amount serotonin reuptake from the synapses.

So what could have potentiated the natural ergot alkaloids in Greece and the Middle East? It could have been a drug known to the Greeks as *moly* (Homer, *The Odyssey,* tr. Rodney Merrill, 2002, 210–215) and to others as wild rue or Syrian rue. Wild rue contains harmaline, the same beta carboline as the potentiating component in *ayahuasca.*

In the Hellenistic and Roman periods wild rue may have proliferated throughout the Middle East, especially along the camel caravan trails. David Flattery has argued that wild rue was the sole sacred plant known as *soma* and *haoma* to the ancient Indo-Europeans (Flattery 1989, 36). The difficulty with this theory is that those who ingest extracts from this plant may attain calm elation, but unless they take an almost toxic dose, they do not hallucinate (Gracie and Zarkov 1986, Shulgin and Shulgin 1997).

The religious importance of wild rue is that if combined with a hallucinogen, it can greatly potentiate the latter. The amateur chemists Gracie and Zarkov reported that Syrian (wild) rue seeds can boost the potency of LSD three or fourfold. After ingesting it they felt tremendous elation (Gracie and Zarkov 1985, 1986).

Was this the great secret of Eleusis: the combination of two drugs, in exact proportions, neither of which alone would have been able to produce a great mental high?

If this hypothesis is to have any relevance to Christianity, then both ergot and wild rue would have had to be available in Palestine in the first century C.E.

In the first century C.E. Dioscorides, a Greek botanist who lived in Cilicia (southeastern Asia Minor, just north of present-day Syria), identified a bush that was already known in Iran, Egypt and Greece and had spread to the Levant. Dioscorides called it *Peganon agrion.* Today it is known in Western botany as *Peganum harmala* or wild rue, Syrian rue, African rue, etc. The Arabs call it *harmal;* the Iranians call it *espand.* Dioscorides considered wild rue as a more effective but also more dangerous medicine than common rue, a similar plant without psychoactive properties (Gunther 1934, 186–190).

The herb "rue" (*peganon*) is mentioned once in the New Testament. In Luke 11:43, Jesus says:

> But woe to you, Pharisees! For you tithe mint and rue [*peganon*] and herbs of all kinds, and neglect justice and the love of God; it is those you ought to have practiced, without neglecting the others.

Jesus did not disapprove of the tithing of mint and rue unless it caused neglect of justice and the love of God (*The New Oxford Annotated Bible,* 3rd ed., 2001).

From this context it seems that "rue" was considered to be a valuable herb. Biblical scholars usually interpret *peganon* to mean common rue, a questionable translation. Mint is a remedy for mild nausea. Common rue does not cause nausea. Wild rue *does* cause mild nausea. Mint linked with "rue" may be a pointer to the interpretation of the Luke's rue as wild rue.

The Jewish historian Flavius Josephus (37–100 C.E.) told of a large plant northeast of the Dead Sea called *ba'aras* that "emitted" a brilliant light toward evening. The name came from the Hebrew root *ba'ar*, to burn. It was used by healers "to drive out demons." Demons who took "possession" of someone were blamed for mental illness (Josephus 1988, Book 7, Chapter Six and Three). Irene and Walter Jacob suggested that this plant was *Peganum harmala* (Jacob 1993, 100–101). If true, the plant could serve as an anti-depressant.

Wild rue is a bright green perennial succulent, resistant to drought (Flattery 1989, 38 and Appendix). Its stems form concentric fans, with white flowers of radial symmetry growing at the tip of each stem. These flowers take the form of a pentacle, a magic symbol in Europe and the official symbol of the Wiccan religion today (Bannerjee 2007).

The fruit of wild rue forms and ripens in late summer or fall. The golden trefoil-shaped seed pods contain about fifty reddish brown triangular seeds. The seeds and roots, when crushed in a hand mortar and then boiled, yield the alkaloid harmaline. The amount of the psychoactive element in mature seeds is 2–7% and in roots, 1.4%–3.2%. To get the psychoactive effect, 5–10 grams of seeds, or 10–30 grams of roots are necessary (Flattery 1989, 33; Winkelman 2000, 210; Most 1985).

When the dried bush is burned it gives off a musky, pleasant fragrance. In the folk belief of Arabs and Iranians today the burning of the dried plant is thought to ward off the effects of the Evil Eye. It is burned as incense at Persian weddings and other festive occasions.

The seeds of wild rue are very bitter. Those ingesting them must find something sweet to offset their bitterness. Honey was the principal sweetener in ancient times. The priestesses at Eleusis were beekeepers and bore the name *melissae,* bees. The alternative was honeydew.

The early Christians could have harvested the seeds of wild rue in the fall, stored them in a dry place, and then combined them with ergots in the spring for Easter and Pentecost celebrations.

In addition, from wild rue a dark red / purple dye called "Turkey red" can be extracted and used in making oriental carpets and fezzes (Flattery 1989, 36 and 43). This color is similar to that in the sclerotia of the fungus *Claviceps purpurea.* The coincidence may have led to experimentation with the two sources of red dye. Red wine can also be used as a dye, as anyone who has spilled it on a light carpet knows. A sacred drink made from ergot and wild rue would have had much the same red color and the same dyeing property. Like wine, it too would have symbolized blood and thus life itself.

In modern Iran and its environs, where New Year is celebrated at the spring equinox, a drink called *haoma* or *para haoma* [partial *haoma*] is served. Although non-hallucinogenic, some of its ingredients call to mind the drink described above: 1) pomegranate juice, which is red like the juice of wild rue; 2) an ephedrine compound, which is a stimulant and substitutes for a hallucinogen; and 3) goat's milk, which may be contaminated with *Claviceps paspali* in the spring (Strausberg 2008, 86). Thus the contemporary New Year's drink resembles its more potent predecessor.

Conclusion

The evidence presented here suggests that some of the visions in the New Testament, and the apocalyptic thinking associated with them, were the result of the ingestion of a hallucinogenic drink.

The "transfiguration" of Jesus, the sudden conversion of Paul, and the role of the shepherds and Magi are no longer discrepant, but serve to support a new and perhaps more plausible explanation of the origins of Christianity.

Zoroastrianism influenced the Jews in general and Jesus in particular. The moralization of religion, the linearization of a morally significant religious narrative, light symbolism in the New Testament, and apocalyptic thinking were all borrowed from Zoroastrian sources. It is at least plausible that Jesus and his disciples on certain occasions made use of a hallucinogenic drink.

References

Aaronson, Bernard, and Humphrey Osmond, eds. *Psychedelics.* New York: Anchor. 1970.

Alatrash, G. et al. 2006. "Rhabdomyolysis after ingestion of foxy, a hallucinogen," *Mayo Clinic Proceedings* 81 (4), 550–551.

Allison, Dale C. 2005. "Jesus." *Encyclopedia of Religion,* vol. 7, 4843–4852.

Arcamone, F., et al. 1960. "Production of lysergic acid derivatives by a strain of *Claviceps paspali* Stevens and Hall in submerged cultures, *Nature* letter 187 (July 16), 238–239.

———. 1999. "The Eschatology of Jesus." *The Encyclopedia of Apocalypticism,* ed. Dale C. Allison, vol. 1, 267–302. New York: Continuum.

Bannerjee, Neela. 2007. "Wiccans Keep the Faith in Religion Under Wraps." *New York Times,* May 16.

Borg, Jacqueline, et al. 2003. "The serotonin system and spiritual experiences." *American Journal of Psychiatry* 160, 1965–1969.

Boyce, Mary, ed. and tr. 1984. *Textual Sources for the Study of Zoroastrianism.* Chicago: University of Chicago Press.

CAB International. 1984. *Distribution Maps of Plant Diseases.* Map 90, *Claviceps paspali.* www.cabi.org.

Cherian, A., and M. Maguire. 2005. "Transient blindness following intravenous ondansetron." *Anaesthesia* 60:9, 938–939.

Collins, John J., et al., eds. 1998. *Encyclopedia of Apocalyptism*, vol. 1. New York: Continuum.

———. 2005. "Apocalypse. " *Encyclopedia of Religion*, vol. 1, 409–419.

Coogan, Michael D., ed. 2001. *The New Oxford Annotated Bible* (NRSV). 3rd ed. Oxford: Oxford University Press.

Dewhurst, Kenneth, and A. W. Beard. 1970. "Sudden religious conversion in temporal lobe epilepsy." *British Journal of Psychiatry* 117, 497–507.

Dobkin de Rios, Marlene, and Oscar Janiga. 2003. *LSD, Spirituality, and the Creative Process.* Rochester, Vermont: Park Street Press.

Ehrman, Bart D. 2005. *Misquoting Jesus.* San Francisco: Harper.

Enzel, Y., et al. 2003. "Late Holocene climates of the Near East deduced from Dead Sea level variations and modern regional winter rainfall." *Quaternary Research* 60:3, 263–273.

Flattery, David. 1989. *Haoma and Harmaline.* Berkeley: University of California Press.

Fox, George. 1911. *Journal.* 2 vols. Cambridge: Cambridge University Press.

"Frankincense." Wikipedia. See also the journal of the FASEB, *Journal of the Societies for Experimental Biology,* May 2008.

Funk, Robert, et al. eds. 1993. *The Five Gospels: The Search for the Authentic Words of Jesus.* New York: Scribners.

Garsoïan, Nina. 1997. "The Emergence of Armenia." *The Armenian People,* ed. Richard Hovannisian, vol. 2. New York: St. Martins. 37–62.

Goldreich, Zair. 2003. *The Climate of Israel.* New York: Kluwer Academic/Plenum.

Gracie and Zarkov. 1985. "Three beta-carboline containing plants as potentiators of synthetic DMT and other indole psychedelics." Erowid Vault, erowid.org.

———. 1986. "Peganum harmala: An Indo-European plant teacher." Erowid Vault, erowid.org.

Greene, Mott T. 1992. *Natural Knowledge in Pre-Classical Antiquity.* Baltimore: Johns Hopkins.

Griffiths, R. R. et al. 2006. "Psilocybin can occasion mystical type experiences having substantial and sustained personal meaning and spiritual significance," *Psychopharmacology* 187:268–283.

Grof, Stanislav, M.D. 1975. *Realms of the Human Unconscious; Observations of LSD Research.* New York: Viking.

Gunther. Robert T. 1934. *The Greek Herbal of Dioscorides.* Oxford: Oxford University Press.

Henderson, Leigh H., and William Glass. *LSD: Still With Us After All Those Years.* 1994. New York: Lexington Books.

Hillman, D.C.A. 2008. *The Chemical Muse: Drug Use and the Roots of Western Civilization.* New York: St. Martins.

Hofmann, Albert. 1986. *Persephone's Quest: Entheogens and the Origins of Religion,* ed. R. Gordon Wasson et al. New Haven: Yale University Press. 31–34.

Homer. 2002. *The Odyssey*, tr. Rodney Merrill. Ann Arbor: University of Michigan Press.

Jacob, Irene and Walter, eds. 1993. *The Healing Past; Pharmaceuticals in the Biblical and Rabbinic World.* Studies in Ancient Medicine, vol. 7. Leiden: Brill.

Jay, Mike. 1999. *Blue Tide: The Search for Soma.* Brooklyn, N.Y.: Autonomedia.

Josephus, Flavius. 1988. *The Works of Josephus. The Wars of the Jews*, tr. William Whiston. Peabody, Mass.: Hendrickson Press.

Leary, Timothy. 1968. *High Priest.* Berkeley: Ronin.

Lee, Martin A., and Shlain, Bruce. *Acid Dreams: The CIA, LSD, and the Sixties' Rebellion.* New York: Grove Press.

Mahmoudian, Massoud, et al. 2002. "Toxicity of *Peganum harmala.*" *Iranian J. of Pharmacology and Therapeutics*, 11:1, 1–4.

Matossian, Mary. 2007. "Why the Quakers Quaked." *Quaker History* 96:1, 36–51.

Most, Albert. 1985. *Peganum Harmala: The Hallucinogenic Herb of the American Southwest.* (Denton, Texas: Venom Press) Erowid. org.

Nichols, David E. 2004. "Hallucinogens." *Pharmacology and Therapeutics* 101:2, 131–181.

Pahnke, W. N. 1969. "Psychedelic drugs and mystical experience." *International Psychiatry Clinics* 5,149–162.

Pootanakit, K., and William Jay Brunken. 2001. "Identification of 5HT (3A) and 5HT (3B) receptor subunits in mammalian retinae: Potential pre- and synaptic modulation of photo receptors." *Brain Research* 896, 77–85.

Rosen, Arlene Miller. 2007. *Civilizing Climate. Social Responses to Climate Change in the Ancient Middle East.* London: Altamira.

Rudgley, Richard. 1988. *The Encyclopedia of Psychoactive Substances.* New York: St. Martins-Griffin. 24–30.

Russell, James R. 1987. *Zoroastrianism in Armenia.* Cambridge, Mass.: Harvard University, Department of Near Eastern Languages and Civilizations.

Satora, L., et al. 2005. "Poisoning resulting from the ingestion of magic mushrooms in Krakow." *Przegi Lek* 62:6, 394–396.

Schiff, P. L. 2006. "Ergot and its Alkaloids." *American Journal of Pharmacological Education* 70:5, 98.

Shulgin, Alexander, and Ann Shulgin. 1997. "Harmaline." *Tryptamines I Have Known and Loved: The Chemistry Continues* [TiHKAL: The Continuation]. Berkeley, Calif.: Transform Press.

Siegel, Ronald K., and M. E. Jarvik. 1975. "Drug-induced hallucinations in animals and man." In *Hallucinations: Behavior, Experience, and Theory,* ed. R. K. Siegel and L. J. West. New York: Wiley. 81–161.

Stannard, Jerry. 1999. "The plant called *moly,*" *Herbs and Herbalism in the Middle Ages and Renaissance.* Aldershot, Hampshire, U.K.: Ashgate.

Strausberg, Michael. 2008. *Zarathustra and Zoroastrianism.* London: Equinox.

Valencic, Ivan. 1994. "Has the mystery of the Eleusinian Mysteries been solved?" *Yearbook for Ethnomedicine and the Study of Consciousness* 3. 325–336. Schaffer Library of Drug Policy, www.druglibrary.org.

Villablanca, J. and Riobo, F. 1970. "Electroencephalographic and behavioral effects of harmaline in intact cats and in cats with chronic mesencephalic transaction," *Psychopharmacology* 17:4, 302–313.

Wasson, Gordon, Albert Hofmann, and Carl Ruck. 1978. *The Road to Eleusis.* New York: Harcourt, Brace, Jovanovich.

Webster, Peter. n.d. "The Secret of the Kykeon." The Psychedelic Library, www.psychedelic-library.org.

Weil, Gunther M., et al. eds. 1965. *The Psychedelic Experience.* New Hyde Park, N.Y.: University Books.

Werblavsky, R. J. Zwi, and Julia Iwerson. 2005. "Light and Darkness." *Encyclopedia of Religion,* 2nd ed., vol. 8, 5450–5455.

Winkelman, Michael. 2000. *Shamanism: The Neural Ecology of Consciousness and Healing.* Westport, Conn.: Bergen and Garvey.

Conclusion

The development of religion in Europe and the Middle East may have been shaped in part by psychoactive drugs. This book traces the history of four such drugs and their sources: the ergot fungus *Claviceps paspali* (a source of the hallucinogen LSD), the wild rue *Paganum harmala,* the opium poppy *Papaver somniferum,* and the wine grape *Vitis vinifera.*

Brains stimulated by psychoactive drugs may have produced the images of supernatural beings found in religious records. According to researchers such as Johns Hopkins University behavioral biologist Ronald Griffiths, hallucinogens can not only relieve painful psychological symptoms but also produce profoundly meaningful, even blissful, experiences. Some research subjects were convinced of the reality of these experiences and remembered the bliss they conveyed (John Tierney, "Hallucinogens Have Doctors Tuning In Again," *New York Times,* April 10, 2011).

Psychoactive drugs, producing rapture, and figures in the starry sky, inspiring awe, were powerful influences on ancient religion. For those who experienced it, rapture compelled belief, and the memory of rapture was powerful, deep, and lasting. The starry skies were a regular reminder of the magnificence and eternal duration of the world.

INDEX

B

D

E

F

G

H

I

J

K

L

M

N

Q

R

Y

Z

About the Author

Los Angeles native Mary Kilbourne Matossian was born in 1930 to Norman Kilbourne, M.D., a Yale honor graduate, and the former Katharine Hillix, a YWCA secretary.

At age seventeen, Mary received a scholarship to Stanford University, from which she graduated in 1951 *magna cum laude* and Phi Beta Kappa. The following year, as a Rotary Fellow, she attended the American University of Beirut (Lebanon), receiving her M.A. in Near Eastern History, then returned to Stanford, where she completed her Ph.D. in History in 1955.

In 1954 Mary married Garo Matossian, an Armenian physician whom she had met in Beirut. They moved to Boston in the fall of 1956, where Garo received advanced medical training at the Lahey Clinic. While affiliated with the Russian Research Center at Harvard, Mary revised her dissertation on Soviet Armenia for publication. She taught History at the University of Maryland for 31 years.

Mary Matossian is the author of *Shaping World History: Breakthroughs in Ecology, Technology, Science, and Politics* (M. E. Sharpe, 1997); *Poisons of the Past: Molds, Epidemics, and History* (Yale University Press, 1989); *Armenian Village Life Before 1914* (with Susie Hoogasian Villa, Wayne State University Press, 1982); and *The Impact of Soviet Policies in Armenia* (Brill, 1962). Among her scholarly articles, those which foreshadow the themes in this book include "Ergot and the Salem Witchcraft Affair" (*American Scientist,* 1982), and "Symbols of Seasons and the Passage of Time: Barley and Bees in the New Stone Age" (*Griffith Observer,* 1980).

CPSIA information can be obtained at www.ICGtesting.com
Printed in the USA
LVOW04*1535180115

423350LV00008B/79/P

9 781626 529342